Happy Father's Day
Love, Ward
2002

The Journey To Our Future

The History of Hickman Mills C-1 School District 1902-2002

The Journey to Our Future

The History of Hickman Mills C-1 School District 1902-2002

This book was created on behalf of the Hickman Mills C-1 School District, Kansas City, Missouri, as part of the Centennial Celebration project.

BY JAMI PARKISON

Cover: The 5 original schools in Hickman Mills C-1 School District: center, first Ruskin High School; clockwise from top left, Hickman School; Holmes Park School; Union Point School; Rockford School

First Edition

For information write:
Hickman Mills C-1 School District
9000 Old Santa Fe Road
Kansas City, MO 64138

Cataloging-in-Publication Data
Jami Parkison
The Journey To Our Future
The History of the Hickman Mills C-1 School District, 1902 - 2002
by Jami Parkison
Library of Congress Control Number: 2002102334
ISBN 0-9664470-7-7
1. Hickman Mills C-1 School District – Missouri – Kansas City – History
Schools – Education – Midwest

10 9 8 7 6 5 4 3 2 1

Contents

The 2001-2002 Board of Education for the Hickman Mills C-1 School District, Kansas City, Missouri: front row, left to right, Dr. Margorie Williams (Superintendent), Teresa Edens, Mattie Johnson, Bonnie Whyte, Mildred E. Harness (Secretary); back row, Roscoe Bernard, George Flesher, Scott Jennings, David Odneal.

PREFACE

This proud and venerable school district was built with great vision. Now, 100 years later, we continue that vision, which is the cornerstone of our school district – to educate for a lifetime of learning.

It is an honor to be a part of the 100 year celebration of the Hickman Mills C-1 School District. As a product of the school system, a parent, a Board of Education member and a longstanding member of the community, I take particular pride in introducing the publication of the book of our history, *The Journey to Our Future – The History of the Hickman Mills C-1 School District, 1902-2002.*

My family moved into the Hickman Mills area in the early 1950s. I have lived through the tornado, the growth, teacher strikes, split sessions, budget crunches, school closings and reopenings and the current growth of our district and the area.

As a student of history, I am proud of the rich traditions of the Ruskin and Hickman Mills areas. Our strength is in our ability to meet the needs of all our children. The Hickman Mills C-1 School District has evolved from a rural community to a vital and diverse urban setting, which sets high academic standards and a nurturing of our most treasured resource – our children.

I have lived through much of the history of the district and am proud to call the Hickman Mills area my home. The spirit of Edwin Hickman, one of the first settlers of the area, and his keen awareness of the value of education are evident today in all our District schools. Mr. Hickman can take pride today – 100 years after his dream – that the educational vision he had for his children has been carried on and will continue to live in our children for the next 100 years.

George Flesher,
President
Hickman Mills C-1 School District
Board of Education

"When skill and
love work together,
expect a masterpiece."

– John Ruskin

Dr. Marjorie Williams, Superintendent, Hickman Mills C-1 School District

INTRODUCTION

Through the enchantment of history, the Hickman Mills C-1 School District is able to re-live our past and visualize our future. We can capture the true essence of the times in which our predecessors lived, and utilize our imaginations to better understand the challenges they faced.

As we embark on our 100-year celebration, we are excited for the opportunity to bring our history alive through manuscript and pictures. Our hope is that this book will provide you a visual journey from our past to our present. The Hickman Mills School District is rich with stories shared from our historic Three Trails to our current economic development in the community.

Our journey begins in the community where each one of you plays an integral part. That community is best illustrated as a carefully woven tapestry in which each thread signifies the many generations of students, teachers, administrators, parents and community leaders who have served our school district and contributed to its many strengths. These past generations have helped point the way to our future — a future that continues to prosper by everyone working together for a common purpose. Our purpose has been, and always will be, strong communities building strong schools.

Earlier this year, we promised to design a document that would capture the history of the Hickman Mills School District. The promise has been fulfilled, and I am sure that you will delight in this publication. As superintendent of schools, it is a rewarding opportunity to be a part of this historical journey, rich in culture and quality educational programs.

I hope you enjoy the journey!

Dr. Marjorie Williams,
Superintendent of Schools
Hickman Mills C-1 School District

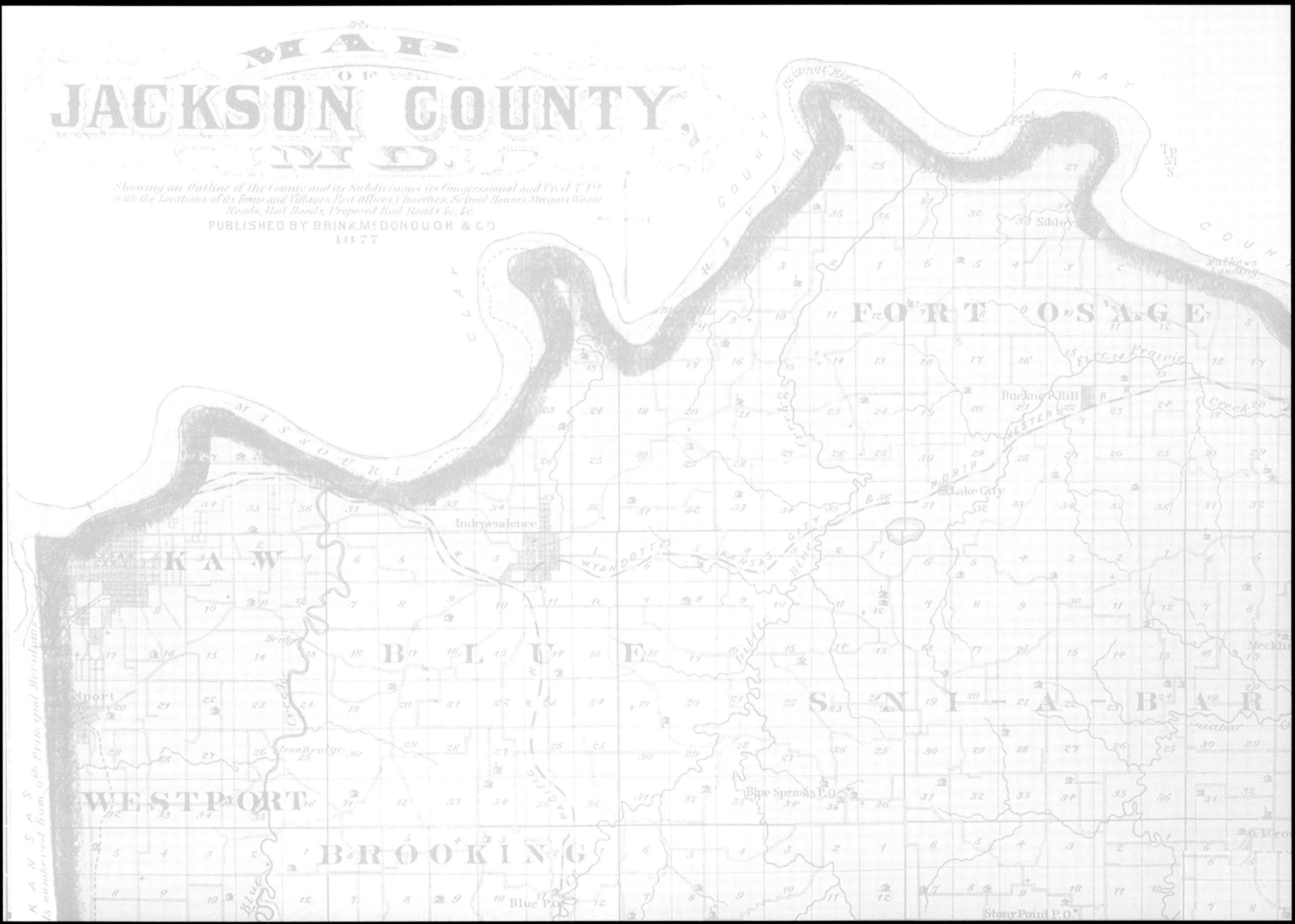

Chapter 1: The Journey's Roots

THE LAND

The journey begins with the land. In prehistoric times, a series of glaciers, moving from today's Canada, shoved massive rocks and rich topsoil southward across the heart of the North American continent. When the ice sheets receded, the Missouri River system filled in the cracks. Along the southern edge of the last glacier, a wedge of fertile prairie, covered in tall grass and almost treeless, spread out high above two large rivers, later called the Big Blue and Little Blue.

From the beginning, the land was prized real estate. Native Americans, who first arrived ten thousand years ago, hunted buffalo here as the herds migrated across the prairie. The high ridge provided an excellent lookout for the Osage tribes, who lived in the area well into the 19th century.

With the Louisiana Purchase in 1803, the U.S. claimed ownership of 828,000 square miles in the heart of the continent. In June, 1804, Merriwether Lewis and William Clark, commissioned by President Thomas Jefferson to explore the new territory, arrived near the great bend in the Missouri River. "This bluff," wrote Clark in his journal, "will be a good site for a fort trading house with the Indians."

The site became Fort Osage. As a factory [the name used for a government-trading agency], the fort offered the Osage protection from enemy tribes and the opportunity to trade with private fur companies. The Osage occupied a 24-mile-wide strip of land

According to the Smithsonian Institute's archaeologist, J. Mett Shippe, ancient artifacts unearthed in the Kansas City area – arrow and spear points and other stone tools – revealed that Indians may have lived here as long ago as 10,000 years. A culture known as Mississippian lived in Jackson County between 800-1300 A.D. After that date, no evidence of a permanent and long-standing Native American community has been found, although the Missouri, Osage [the illustration shows an Osage warrior] and Kansa tribes continued to hunt here and to maintain villages within 50 miles.

The French first encountered the Osage of Missouri in the 1670s. The tribe became fur trading business partners with the French. The Europeans sold the Indians guns and horses, thus allowing the tribe to dominate the area for more than a century. In 1755, the Osage helped the French defeat British General Edward Braddock's army. When the French influence faded from Missouri, the Osage, always adaptable, quickly established relations with the Spanish and finally with Americans after the U.S. purchased the Louisiana Territory.

From 1877 *Illustrated Historical Atlas of Jackson Co., Missouri*

The first European explorer to push deep into the American continent was a Spaniard named Francisco Coronado. In 1541, he and his 1,000 men traveled from Mexico, coming as far north as a spot about five miles from today's Dodge City, Kansas, before turning back toward the southwest.

One hundred and forty one years later (1682), Sieur de LaSalle claimed for France the central portion of today's United States. It was an area called the Louisiana Territory and included the Hickman Mills C-1 School District. In 1763, the territory was ceded to Spain, which ceded the land back to France in 1800. Once again, on April 30, 1803, the massive territory changed hands when the Louisiana Purchase became the first territorial acquisition by the United States. It added land between the Mississippi River and the Rocky Mountains. On May 14, the same year, Merriwether Lewis and William Clark and an expedition team set out from St. Louis to explore the new territory. That summer, the Corps of Discovery arrived at the great bend in the Missouri River, at its confluence with the Kaw, and the future site of Kansas City.

along the river, an area encompassing most of today's Jackson County. Because it was Indian territory, the land attracted few permanent white settlers until the fort closed in 1822.

Besides the fort's closure, several other events encouraged settlement. The first was the admission of Missouri into the Union as the 24th state in 1821. The second, occurring in the same year, was William Becknell's extraordinarily profitable trading trip down the Santa Fe Trail from Missouri to the southwest, a region occupied by the Spanish empire. The third was the 1825 Council Grove treaty in which the Osage and Kansa Indians ceded their land in Missouri to the United States. The following year, the Missouri General Assembly approved a new county, named for a war hero and western idol, Andrew Jackson.

With statehood status, the allure of riches in Santa Fe and the removal of native residents, the path was clear for unimpeded settlement. And for the rest of the century, and well into the 20th century, Jackson County became a beacon for immigrants. Some were just passing through, on their way to riches or adventure in the American west. Others came to live here, first along the Missouri River and then onto the fertile prairie land left by the glaciers.

By the 1830s an area in southwest Jackson County was a popular destination for travelers intent on settling Missouri. An 1881 history of Jackson County described this high ground between the Big Blue and Little Blue rivers: "the soil of rich loam covers the rock from a depth of a few feet to twenty feet and not a tree could be seen for miles on the prairie."

The settlers on this rich prairie land, though few, were well established by the mid 1830s. The birth of the first white child, named Thomas Flanery, was recorded in 1837. The following year Mr. and Mrs. Robert Pierson became the first white couple married there.

Most people who settled southwest Jackson County came from southern states, especially Kentucky, Virginia and Tennessee. Many were slave owners. Such a man was

One of Elizabeth and Charles Jefferys' eight children, Edward, recalled, "He and mother [shown here] had both been impressed by [Nathaniel] Hawthorne's Blithedale Romance, published in 1852, six years before their marriage, the story of a socialized community for the betterment of mankind. Father's Blithedale was of the most fertile soil, containing forests of black walnut and watered by two small rivers, the Big and the Little Blue. He secured for his stock farm, the finest stock obtainable. From Spain he imported a jackass at great cost for the raising of `Missouri Mules,' as famous then as they have been since. His stallion and bull were thoroughbreds. The cows and mares were of the best strains."

When the Frisco Railroad built a depot in Hickman Mills, the land was given by the family in 1899 on the condition that the station be called "Jefferys." The station, built on Red Bridge Road between today's Highway 71 and Grandview Road, was maintained with an agent and telegraph service until about 1914, when the building burned. Afterwards, mail was still carried on the train, but passengers at the station platform had to flag the train to stop. When mail service converted to truck delivery around 1954, passenger service was discontinued.

Photograph courtesy of the Hickman Mills Community Christian Church.

Charles Jefferys, born in Belgium and heir to a fortune built up in the British West Indies..

Soon after marrying Elizabeth Miller, his boss's daughter, in 1858, Jefferys, a 27-year-old civil engineer, purchased land between the Blue and Little Blue rivers. County records for 1859 show that the property included 13 tracts ranging from 40 to 760 acres and totaling more than 1,800 acres. The price was $17,300. One tract of 95 acres included this notation: "minus one road and 12 acres for a mill," probably referring to the land owned by Edwin Hickman, the local miller, and the public road, which is now Red Bridge Road. (The Jefferys' land included much of today's Hickman Mills C-1 School District. Ruskin High School sits in the center of the largest portion of the Jefferys' property.)

Using slave and immigrant labor, Jefferys built two large homes, calling them Hawthorne and Blithedale. Jefferys' farm manager, Jacob Palmer, later described Blithedale: "splendidly furnished, everything in it was of best quality. There were paintings done by the old Masters, for which Mr. Jefferys had a standing offer of $14,000. There were other valuable paintings, glass cases of curiosities gathered by travel in foreign lands, statues, Swiss carvings and bric-a-brac. In the library were wagonloads of costly books and engravings, and other statuary and pictures. Two pearl handled rapiers were crossed above a picture of Bonaparte..." Both Jefferys' mansions played key roles in the history of the region.

Jefferys, a rich man, was unusual. Most who settled the land had modest means. What they brought to the American west was a determination to prosper in a strange and uncertain land. Despite the glowing 1881 report of "soil of rich loam," the land was almost unyieldingly hard, having never been tilled. For many years the early settlers required a four- to eight-team of oxen to pull a barshear plow [a saw-blade steel, invented in the 1830s expressly to cut through tough western sod] through the packed soil. And even that labor was followed by hacking the rock-like chunks with an ax.

And so the land, tens of thousands of years in the making, became the crucible on which a special breed of people, unswervingly self-assured and optimistic, could build for their children and their children's children a legacy – one that would last a century and beyond.

In 1818, the Territory of Missouri, which was part of the Louisiana Purchase, applied for admission to the Union. Slavery was legal in the Territory of Missouri, and about 10,000 slaves lived there. Most people expected Missouri to become a slave state. When the bill to admit Missouri to the Union was introduced, there were 11 free states and 11 slave states, which meant free states and slave states each had 22 U.S. Senators. Missouri's admission threatened to destroy this balance.

Rep. James Tallmadge of New York proposed an amendment to Missouri's statehood bill that would prohibit bringing any more slaves into Missouri and would grant freedom to the children of slaves born within the state after its admission. Southerners feared Tallmadge's amendment was just a harbinger of national legislation against slavery. Although the Tallmadge amendment passed the House, it was defeated in the Senate. Had it passed the Senate, slave-holding settlers such as Jefferson Johnson and Charles Jefferys would never have come to Jackson County.

During the next session of Congress, Maine applied for admission to the Union. This gave lawmakers the chance to maintain the pro- and anti-slavery balance. And so the "Missouri Compromise" was born on March 3, 1820. Temporarily settling the debate over slavery, the law admitted Maine as a free state and authorized Missouri to form a state constitution, which permitted slavery. The compromise also banned slavery from the Louisiana Purchase north of the southern boundary of Missouri, the line of 36 degrees 30 minutes north latitude – except in the state of Missouri itself.

Before Congress admitted Missouri in 1821 as the 24th state, a second Missouri Compromise was necessary. Henry Clay, the Speaker of the House, helped work out this agreement that prohibited the Missouri legislature from denying black citizens, as distinguished from slaves, their constitutional rights.

One hundred years after Charles Jefferys built his two mansions, his great grandson, also named Charles Jefferys, described the houses during a speech he delivered to the Old Settlers Club in Hickman Mills: "fine Victorian homes of about 16 rooms... The main house, Blithedale [shown here], torn down in the 1920s, was situated about 500 feet north of what is now Longview Road [today the road is at 115th but at the time of this speech it ran along 111th Street before turning south a little east of Hickman Mills] and Orchard Road...[Hawthorne] was...situated at the northwest corner of Craig [107th Street] and Blue Ridge Roads. The latter was destroyed by fire."

A large stone wall about 15 miles in length bordered the property and stood until the mid 20th century. According to a 1969 article in The Kansas City Star, *the stone wall was four to six feet high, "quarried at a distance by men brought over from Europe, and taken to the farm by ox teams. Stone from these fences was used in macadamizing Blue Ridge Boulevard at the turn of the century. The last of the old fencing just north of Ruskin High School was razed in 1953 to make way for new homes."*

THE TRAILS

Eastward I go only by force; but westward I go free. I must walk toward Oregon and not toward Europe. Henry David Thoreau.

Whether passing through or staying to settle permanently, the streams of travelers coming to the western frontier via Jackson County moved along three trails: the Santa Fe, California and Oregon. During the 19th century, the routes of the trails shifted, in large part depending on changes in private property boundaries.

Settlements in Jackson County, the eastern terminus during the 60-year histories of the three great trails, naturally grew up along those highways. Consequently one of the first areas to be settled was Washington Township, in southwest Jackson County. Organized in February 1836, the township served as one of the earliest principal routes for the three trails. After 1850, when Kansas City, Missouri, was founded, the routes moved primarily along the northwestern and western side of the county.

Western migration received an enormous boost in 1845. That year James K. Polk became president, winning on a platform promoting the doctrine of Manifest Destiny. The expansionist policy, originally expressed by John O'Sullivan, editor of the *United States Magazine and Democratic Review*, stated that it was "our manifest destiny to overspread the continent allotted by Providence for free development of our yearly multiplying millions." Overspreading meant moving westward, and at that time Missouri was the Union's most western state – the gateway to destiny.

Edwin Alfred Hickman was born in 1819 to William B. Hickman, an orphan who prospered in Kentucky and Virginia during the late 1700s, and his second wife. William became a national leader in the Baptist church and his portrait hangs in the Cabildo Museum, a state archive in New Orleans.

The 12-year-old Edwin was apprenticed to James Shannon, a harness maker in Frankfort, Kentucky, where he helped make saddle bags for the government. In 1840, Edwin rode horseback from Kentucky to Independence, Missouri, where he joined older half-brothers, already living in the state.

Edwin taught school for six years. In 1845 he married Catherine Oldham. He then built a saw and grist mill near Independence, Missouri.

When wood became scarce around Independence, Edwin bought 40 acres in Washington Township. He purchased a plot along a creek, ideal for building a steam-powered mill, from Randall Allen who had already laid out a townsite in 1845. Machinery for the mill came from factories in Pittsburg, hauled down the Ohio River, the Mississippi and Missouri Rivers and finally carried along the Santa Fe Trail. Some historians believe that the spur connecting the trail to Hickman's mill ran from Palestine Cemetery (Old Santa Fe Road and 93rd Street), then south along today's Bennington to Red Bridge Road.

Photograph courtesy of the Hickman Mills Community Christian Church.

Hickman Mills Community Christian Church, originally established in 1845 near 87th and Raytown Road, is the third oldest Christian church in Jackson County. On the list of its first members are the names of four people with the inscription "colored" printed beside each. These four people were slaves of one of the church members. The first church built on the land donated by Edwin Hickman was a frame construction with a long uncovered porch on the front. There were two front doors, one for men and the other for women. Hitching posts for horses and buggies were in the front. Nearby were mounting blocks for children and infirm adults.

In 1896 a second frame building was constructed to accommodate the 75 parishioners. Larger and more ornate, the second church included a vestibule and a belfry with a short steeple. Within 30 years attendance more than doubled and a third church was built on the site. Completed in December 1929, the new church, shown here and which is still standing, was built of stone. The Norman-Gothic design received an award from the Kansas City chapter of the American Institute of Architecture. The building also received first prize from the church architecture competition sponsored by the Christian Herald. Several master stonemasons from Mexico were hired to create the stone arches in front of the church nave. The educational wing of the church was completed in 1958.

The Missouri River offered the favorite method for traveling to the gateway, although several dirt roads crisscrossed the state. Once a traveler arrived in western Missouri, however, the most practical way to cross the continent was by one of the three overland trails.

The Santa Fe Trail carried primarily commercial traffic. The other two served west-bound settlers. A quarter of a million emigrants traveled the Oregon and California Trails between 1842 and 1870, making it the greatest peacetime migration in the history of the world. Stretching across 2,000 miles, the trip took four to five months. As a result, the trails offered Missouri settlers an array of economic opportunities. Farmers, freighters, millers, manufacturers, wholesalers, wagonmakers, bankers, bakers, traders, trappers, hunters, hustlers and outlaws – all found opportunities in trail traffic.

In 1854, Edwin Hickman moved from Independence and built a steam-powered grist and saw mill along the creek near the intersection of today's Red Bridge Road and Hillcrest Road. Hickman had previously worked in Independence and was aware of the business potential of trail traffic. He believed that a community built in Washington Township, an area bordering the open plains of the Kansas territory, could also capitalize on the migrating market.

But Hickman was thinking beyond just trail trade. A mill, central to any town in those days, could also encourage permanent settlement. For a miller, settlers represented a long-term market. Two years after moving into the township, Hickman donated an acre of land across the road from the mill to the Bethlehem Christian Church, at that time in north Washington Township. The congregation accepted the gift and built a one-room church that eventually became Hickman Mills Community Christian Church. And so a small town, which would grow to become a thriving community during the next century, developed around the mill and the church.

A little more than a year after Pres. James K. Polk's inauguration, in May, 1846, a caravan of travelers headed down the California Trail. They made camp at a site now called Marion Park in the Hickman Mills area. One of the men in the group, Edwin Bryant, wrote in his diary, "14 15 Camped at `Heart [sic] Grove' Jackson County near the Indian line twenty two miles from Independence on the Big blue [sic]."

Bryant was traveling with a caravan later remembered as the Donner Party. The group, which included 20 wagons and a total of 91 people, became stranded in the Sierra Nevada. The trip was plagued by fatal mistakes. When the travelers tried to take a short cut, they lost all of their cattle and oxen, had to abandon many possessions and became snowbound for months in the mountains. One year after beginning their journey, only 47 of the Donner Party came out of the mountains alive, having survived by eating the bodies of their dead comrades.

The grove referred to by Edwin Bryant was Hart Grove, later called Holmes Park where one of the four original schools in C-1 district was built. It was the last place in Missouri where the party stayed before they headed across the Great Plains.

Eight-year-old Patty Reed and her family traveled with the Donner Party. Patty, shown here in later life, was one of the survivors.

After closing the mill in Washington Township, Edwin Hickman went to Colorado to search for gold. In a letter postmarked Georgia Bar, Colorado, October 25, 1860, he wrote his son, "It is the grand object of my life to so raise and educate you Willie and Sis [Anna, his daughter] that you will be a credit to us and useful to yourselves and to society. I think the foundation is laid and nothing but continued effort on your part will accomplish it. Then pay strict attention to your Bible and Christian education and you are safe morally. You are now forming character for all time.

"In the wisdom to the worldly minded, the possession of gold is thought to be the object of our existence but nothing is more delusive. Pure morals, a well educated mind and a good Christian character are as far above the blessing of wealth and the fashions of the day as Heaven is above the Earth."

On August 24, 1857, a nationwide financial panic followed the failure of the New York City branch of the Ohio Life Insurance Company. The panic was due mostly to speculation in railway securities and real estate. As a result, nearly 5,000 businesses failed that year. Another 8,000 failed in 1859.

One of the businesses to fail in 1859 was Hickman's mill. A prosperous and generous man, Hickman had co-signed and guaranteed so many notes for customers and neighbors, who could not meet their obligations after the panic, that the miller was forced to sell his business.

The Waggoner-Gates Milling company in Independence bought Hickman's mill equipment. One of Hickman's neighbors, Solomon Young (Harry S. Truman's great-grandfather) used the building's lumber to construct a barn. A pool, connected to the creek and created for the boiler water as it exited the mill, was the site for church baptisms. Today one of the millstones used to grind grain at Hickman's mill is displayed at the Hickman Mills Community Christian Church.

From 1877 Illustrated Historical Atlas of Jackson Co., Missouri.

O.V. Slaughter, who was a central figure in the consolidation efforts for the Hickman Mills schools, recalled that George S. Hedges was one of the most influential men in the very early years of the community. Hedges' farm is shown here from an illustration appearing in the 1877 atlas of Jackson County. Slaughter wrote that Hedges "came in 1866 and settled one mile south of the mill… Mr. Hedges was a man of dignity, courteous, and a stickler for the refinements. Social affairs at his house were models of good taste in a day when formalities were not observed so strictly. He bought his girls the first piano in Washington Township and had them take lessons."

The Hedges School was built on the farm. It later combined with the Jones School, two miles to the west, to create Hickman School at Longview and Grandview Roads, one of the four original schools in the C-1 district.

The Slaughter family bought the Hedges property after Hedges' death in 1879. Some local historians believe that both Hedges and his wife were buried on land eventually occupied by a large Chevrolet car dealership.

Thomas Flanery and Jefferson Johnson's interest in education was not surprising. Americans have historically placed the pursuit of learning high on their list of imperative rights.

In fact, a cornerstone of any democracy is its determination to make education common to all, even compulsory for all. Although Americans' reluctance to embrace "all" sometimes eclipsed their democratic vision, it is instructive to note that as early as 1647, Massachusetts passed the nation's first major compulsory education law. It mandated that every community with 50 or more families appoint a schoolteacher. In addition, the law required that communities with more than 100 families build a grammar school.

Nearly 140 years later, the Ordinance of 1785 provided the blueprint for establishing settlements by U.S. citizens in territories beyond the original 13 colonies. The congressional act outlined a careful system of grids, called townships, divided into sections and quarter sections (160 acres). Section 16 in the township grid was set aside for residents to build a school. Later this became the familiar pattern for the development of land opened for settlement in the middle west and west, including Jackson County and Washington Township (i.e., the land occupied by Hickman Mills C-1 School District).

Early Schools

The first school in Washington Township was a subscription school, opened in 1840. It was established on the farm of John Flanery, who lived in the northeast part of the township, and whose young son was the first white child born there. Tuition was 10 cents a day, and the first teacher's name was Isaac Crabtree.

Although Missouri's earliest constitution called for the establishment of free schools, the creation of such institutions was impractical in sparsely settled, even turbulent, frontier areas like Jackson County. In fact when the county was organized in 1826, there were few public schools in the nation because an effective public school act was not passed by Congress until 1839, and even then it was many years before a system of public schools could take root and grow.

Washington Township in the early 1800s, indeed the entire western part of the Missouri Territory, was so thinly populated that the early settlers were forced to create small private schools to educate their children. If a parent did not serve as the teacher, the family hired a governess or tutor. Often no more than a single classroom, these learning situations offered a basic grammar-school education.

As rural communities increased in population, two or more families sometimes formed an association for the purpose of educating children. In this system – the subscription school – each child paid tuition to attend. Association members elected a trustee who hired a teacher and found a building or room for classes. A typical subscription school in western Missouri paid the teacher a monthly stipend of one to one and a half-dollars per student. The winter session, which lasted three or four months, was attended by all ages of boys and girls. Only girls and young boys, however, attended the two- to three-month spring session, a time when the older boys worked on the families' farms.

By mid-century, Washington Township was populated sufficiently to sustain the establishment of a privately owned and operated school for higher learning (defined as post-grammar school).

In 1845, Jefferson H. Johnson from Hind County, Mississippi, arrived in Washington Township. An educated man, whose four covered wagons held one of the largest libraries in Jackson County, Johnson organized a grammar school, called the McDonald School District, according to some historians. The next year he opened the Highland Academy on his farm just east of today's Raytown Road and north of 87th Street.

One of the first institutions of higher learning in western Missouri, the academy included a two-story building and several small log cabins used as dormitories. Fifty students attended the school, many coming from other parts of Missouri as well as from other states. When Johnson died in December 1850, his wife, Eliza, took over the school, as well as the family's farm. Highland closed with the outbreak of the Civil War, a bloody conflict that would destroy the lives and fortunes of many people in the tiny settlement around Hickman's Mill.

Chapter 2: The Civil War

PRELUDE TO WAR

In 1849, despite a cholera epidemic in his hometown of St. Louis, Sen. Thomas Hart Benton returned to Missouri from Washington, D.C. He was on a mission, and he was angry.

Since first elected in 1821 when Missouri became a state, Benton had won the hearts and votes of many folks – folks like Edwin Hickman and Jefferson Johnson – who invested their fortunes in property along the Santa Fe Trail in Jackson County. The fiery senator believed that Missouri's future prosperity lay in unrestricted commerce along the trail. A passionate orator, Sen. Benton stood before Congress and, with the drama that earned him the nickname, "Old Roman," he pointed toward the west, toward Missouri, and roared, "THIS is the East. THIS is India."

But twenty-eight years later, a more divisive issue confronted Benton and his Missouri constituents. The issue was slavery, and its corrosive ramifications in Congress penetrated the heart of every problem, every speech. Fiercely anti-slavery and even more fiercely anti-secessionist, Benton compared the endless arguments about slavery with a biblical plague of frogs. "You could not look upon the table but there were frogs, you could not sit down at the banquet but there were frogs, you could not go to the bridal couch and lift the sheets but there were frogs."

In Congress Benton fought against the pro-slavery members of his own party – notably the firebrand from South Carolina, Sen. John C. Calhoun. The lure of gold, discovered at Sutter's Mill a year earlier, prompted Congress to press for California's statehood. But as a free or slave state?

Photograph by John Parkison

The year Hickman's Mill closed (1859), the first Red Bridge was built on the Santa Fe Trail at this site over the Blue River. Nearby was a two-room, brick trading post established in 1833 by Henry Riggs, the post's builder and operator. Riggs traded primarily with members from the Osage and Kansa tribes until the Indians were forcibly resettled in Kansas Territory. Also near this river crossing was David Tate's farm, the site of a battle between William Quantrill's raiders and the Federals. The first Red Bridge remained standing until 1892, when a second bridge was built about 300 yards south. The present steel and concrete Red Bridge was constructed in 1932 on the same site.

To complicate matters, Missouri's pro-slavery legislature adopted a resolution directing the state's representatives in Congress to take a firm stand for slavery. Benton was outraged. He told his St. Louis audiences, "I shall be found in the right place – on the side of my country and the Union."

Benton found few supporters in his hometown, and even fewer in western Missouri. Residents of Jackson County, heavily populated by southerners, recoiled at the idea of granting Union status to abolitionists in the west. Sen. David Atchinson, Missouri's other senator and, like Benton, a Democrat, was chief architect in the successful campaign to defeat the Old Roman in 1851.

Congressional centrists struggled to find some way that the aggrieving sides could co-exist. Born of that desire was the Compromise of 1850. Like the Missouri law thirty years earlier, the new compromise was a give-and-take: California would come in as free, but the admission as free or slave of other states created from territories formerly part of Mexico, including New Mexico and Arizona, would be determined at the ballot box by residents living in the respective territories.

Four years later, the same year Edwin Hickman built his mill, Congress passed the Kansas-Nebraska Act, largely engineered by Missouri's Sen. Atchinson. The 1854 law officially opened Kansas to settlers and allowed the issue of slavery to be decided by voters as each state entered the Union.

Proponents of the 1850 and 1854 measures hoped to settle the debate and calm the anger. It did neither.

What was intended as a lasting rapprochement only served to ignite both sides. Long before Fort Sumter fell to the Confederates, and the Civil War officially began, the fighting along Missouri's frontier borders turned bloody.

Jackson County became a tinderbox. Southern sympathizers were determined to prevent Kansas settlers from voting against slavery. Washington Township – southwest Jackson County – was populated largely by southerners and Confederate sympathizers. By the 1850s, slaveholding was analogous with wealth in Jackson County. Jefferys' vast estate, for example, was built in part with slave labor. In and around Hickman Mills, pro-southern fighters, often called bushwhackers, had no trouble securing sanctuary or obtaining horses, clothes, food, medical attention and information about pro-Union activity. Even children helped by finding small fragments of lead for making bullets. It was here that manpower was found to fill the bushwhackers' ranks. It was here, in the undergrowth along the riverbanks and under cave-like ledges, that the bushwhackers hid out.

Five months after the Kansas-Nebraska law granted sovereignty rights to squatters in western territories, frontier politics, always rowdy, took a decidedly deadly turn. In November 1854, Benton's nemesis, Sen. Atchinson, assembled a gang of border ruffians. Determined to pack the ballot boxes with pro-slavery votes, the senator invaded Kansas.

"The game must be played boldly," Atchinson told a colleague. "If we win, we carry slavery to the Pacific Ocean."

Throughout 1855, an endless stream of southern sympathizers traveled westward to Kansas on trails through Washington Township. Their goal? To populate the territory with pro-slavery voters. Sen. Atchinson, a cheerleader of the movement, told a crowd in St. Joseph, "Enter every election district in Kansas…and vote at the point of a Bowie knife or revolver!" The tactic worked. In Oxford, a little village near today's 97th and State Line Road, for example, the 42 residents cast ballots that mysteriously turned into 1,628 votes.

On May 21, 1856, Atchinson again descended on Kansas with armed supporters. This time he targeted Lawrence, the hotbed of the territory's abolitionism. The senator and his men destroyed the Eldridge Hotel and the newspaper presses. Three days afterwards, in retaliation, abolitionist zealot, John Brown, and seven followers abducted and split open the skulls of five pro-slavery Kansans – none with any links to the Lawrence raid.

And so it began – a relentless pattern of retaliatory bloodletting. For the people of Hickman Mills and other residents in Washington Township, the familiar struggles of turning the prairie into profitable farmland now became a struggle to protect property from armed invaders, to hold the family together – and to stay alive.

WAR

On January 29, 1861, Kansas entered the Union – free. A few weeks later, on March 4, Abraham Lincoln was inaugurated president.

With those two events, all the years of compromise in Washington, D.C. unraveled. The fragile union could not hold. In the early hours of April 12, southern forces attacked and captured Fort Sumter at Charleston, South Carolina. Before the spring could thaw the fields that year in Washington Township, the nation was at war with itself.

Late one night that spring, someone set fire to the Baptist church in the settlement of Rockford, near today's intersection of Raytown and Longview Roads and within the C-1 school district. No one knows who torched the building, the church of many of the township's leaders. Soon afterward the Highland Academy, still run by Eliza Johnson after her husband's death, was burned by abolitionists, also called Jayhawkers.

Some families left the township soon after war was declared. O.V. Slaughter, who later helped found the Hickman Mills C-1 School District, remembered the night his Aunt Sally Rubel and her family hurriedly abandoned their farm and headed west. O.V. was eight years old. The day of their departure, his mother, Amanda, told the boy to find the Rubels' campsite near Harrisonville and to tell the family goodbye. Sometime that night, O.V. crossed paths with Union soldiers. The men wanted to know why the boy was out so late. They suspected him of sneaking supplies to the enemy.

One in eight households in Missouri owned slaves. The vast majority of those slave-holding families lived on rich farmlands along the Missouri and Mississippi River bottoms. Only 36 of Missouri's 114 counties had one thousand or more slaves. Jackson County was one of the 36.

JACKSON COUNTY POPULATION:

Year	Total Population	Free Slaves	Slaves	Slaveholders
1830	2,822	0	193	62
1840	8,466	6	1,361	330*
1850	14,000	41	2,969	[Not available]
1860	22,913	70	3,944	898

**Approximately 30 of these owned 10-20 slaves.)*

Census data from the University of Virginia Library (Website: fisher.lib.virginia.edu/census/)

"My father denied having any knowledge of anything they asked him," O.V.'s son, Stephen, later wrote in the family history, published in 1978. "A rope was put around his neck and the end thrown over a tree limb. The rope was tightened, but still Father denied any knowledge. The leader of the gang then stopped the procedure, said the boy was probably as stupid as he said he was and turned him loose."

In 1902, Jacob Palmer, shown here, farmed the three acres on which the first Ruskin High School was built. During the Civil War, Palmer worked for Charles Jefferys, even after the wealthy landowner fled with his family to Philadelphia.

Palmer recalled that the war years brought constant dangers from unknown sources. One day while working in the fields, he felt "a rifle ball whiz over my head 600 yards from the hedge. I thought that was rather close cutting for a stray shot. When I drew within 15 yards of the fence another ball whizzed by, stinging my ear... I stooped and looked between the top planks of the fence, threw my hand to my hip as if drawing a pistol, intending to ask the fellow what he was shooting at me for, but I saw no one."

Returning from a trip to Olathe, Kansas, Charles Jefferys' farm manager, Jacob Palmer, learned that Jayhawkers planned to murder Jefferys. When Palmer reported the threat to his boss, Elizabeth begged her husband to leave the township. Jefferys, however, was fearful that in his absence the abolitionists would reduce his property to ashes. Consequently, he remained in the area for the next several months, while his wife and children returned to her family in Philadelphia.

A few days before Christmas, 1861, George Searcy, a recent deserter from the Confederate army, robbed several people near Blue Springs, Missouri. On the same day, he also tried to ambush William Quantrill. Quantrill and his men tracked down Searcy and hanged him from a tree along the Little Blue River. The bushwhackers then returned the horses, mules and other property stolen from area residents, including some who were Union sympathizers.

The incident is illuminating. During the war years, there was no law. Sovereignty belonged to the person holding the gun. A man with a weapon was a law unto himself. And viewed by the residents of Jackson County, that at-the-point-of-a-gun law was sometimes the only justice to be found.

Such incidents enhanced the reputation of Quantrill, but the incident that won him the undisputed, though temporary, leadership of the border ruffians took place at a battle in Washington Township.

On March 19, 1862, Gen. Henry Halleck, Union commander of Missouri, issued an order formally condemning all pro-slavery guerillas as outlaws. If captured, they were to be executed. In short, the Union raised the black flag over Missouri.

Four days later, in retaliation for the harsh measure, Quantrill personally executed two men he found on a road just outside Kansas City. One was a Union soldier and one was a bridge toll keeper, killed in front of his young son. After the murders, Quantrill supposedly told his men, who witnessed the event, "Halleck issued the order, but we draw the first blood."

That night Quantrill and about two dozen of his men spent the night at the farmhouse of David Tate in Washington Township, not far from Red Bridge.

Before dawn the next day, a small group of federal troops, scouring the hills of the township for the two men's murderers, surprised the sleeping guerillas.

With his companies of the Second Cavalry in position near Tate's log house, Maj. Samuel Pomeroy called out for the rebels to surrender. One local historian, Harvey Kemper, noted that only two men – brothers named Rollins from Grain Valley, who had joined Quantrill's raiders the day before –

came out with their hands up. The two were shot immediately. (Their bodies remained in Tate's yard until the next day, when they were buried by U.R. Holmes, whose family founded the town of Holmes Park, and later were moved by the Rollins family.)

The raiders and federals exchanged gunfire until finally the Union troops set fire to the house. Anticipating this tactic, Quantrill had searched for an escape route. He found one in the back of the house through weakened sections of logs. Behind the billowing smoke of the torched building, one by one the guerillas escaped.

Later that year, in July, someone stopped at the Jefferys farm and told Jacob Palmer that Henry Younger, father of Cole Younger, had been shot. His body was lying next to his horse and buggy on top of Blue Hill beyond Dodson, a settlement near today's 87th and Paseo. Palmer was asked to bring the body back to Hickman Mills.

"So I hitched a yoke of oxen to a wagon and… went by moonlight to the place and not finding the body, drove on to the farm of Alexander Majors where [I was] informed… that soldiers had taken the body in the direction of Olathe." Palmer returned to Hickman Mills "without meeting anyone on the road, which was, at the time, a much-dreaded probability."

The next month, on August 11, Quantrill and his men captured Independence, Missouri. The action produced a frenzy of raids and counter raids throughout the county. Palmer remembered that in the Hickman Mills area, Jayhawkers descended on residents, robbing and plundering as they went.

Palmer later recalled the local farmers reaction to the Jayhawkers' raid: "Getting some guns that they had hid out, the farmers ran across the fields ahead of the Jayhawkers, ambushed them in a house they were robbing and took them [the Jayhawkers] prisoners. Not having become used to killing, the farmers decided to take their prisoners… and turn them over to the county authorities.

"To make a safe trip they went down the branch and in the thick brush along Heart Grove [Hart Grove] Creek . On their way, they met some of Quantrill's command who inquired what they were doing. When told the circumstances of the situation, the bushwhackers said they would take charge of the prisoners.

William Clarke Quantrill was an opportunist, without strong political or philosophical convictions. Famous as the leader of several hundred pro-southern guerillas, Quantrill arrived in Kansas in 1859, initially teaming with Jayhawkers (pro-Union Kansans) to steal horses and slaves in Missouri. In 1861, when the border war escalated into bloody clashes, Quantrill switched allegiances, gladly filling a leadership vacuum among a group of young Missouri men who hoped to organize against the wanton destructiveness of Jayhawkers. Well-known to residents of Hickman Mills, Quantrill and his pro-Confederate raiders sometimes stopped at the Charles Jefferys estate. Mrs. Jefferys later described Quantrill as a quixotic figure: "He robbed and destroyed but always comported himself debonairly and politely." She remembered one day when Quantrill was about to execute a prisoner in front of Blithedale. She pleaded with the rebel to spare the man's life. Quantrill tipped his hat and made a deep bow. Promising to honor her request, the outlaw rode away with the prisoner. Mrs. Jefferys always believed that as soon as Quantrill was out of her sight, the execution was carried out.

Henry Younger, shown here, operated a dry goods store and farms in Cass and Jackson Counties. He tried to remain neutral during the border wars. When the civil conflict caused widespread hardship in west central Missouri, he invited anyone in need of food – Federals and Confederates – to help themselves to corn from his several cribs. This was a common and practical attitude of many residents. Border war stories abound with anecdotes of families being forced to feed a traveling band of Yankees in the morning and then bushwhackers at night. John Muir, relative of William Muir, one of Union Point's founders, said he was prepared to do anything to survive the dark days of war. "I was determined," he said, "to keep a roof over my family." But Henry Younger's neutrality didn't save him or his family from grief. Most Union authorities and today's historians believe that he was ambushed and killed by Irvin Walley, a Federal militiaman who had a grudge against Cole Younger, Henry's 17-year-old son and one of Quantrill's raiders.

"Quantrill's men took the Jayhawkers men [and] ...went through Mr. Jefferys' big pasture and out at the gate where Ruskin High School now stands. From there they passed into the timber along Little Blue and that is the last that was learned of them."

This story and others like it may account for ghoulish rumors about farmers and hogs occasionally rooting out buried corpses around Hickman Mills and other rural areas after the war.

Quantrill's raid on Independence was nothing compared to his attack on the abolitionist stronghold: Lawrence, Kansas. Some historians believe that a small raiding force assembled at today's Warford Park [between 114th and 119th] prior to joining the other Confederate bushwhackers for the Lawrence raid.

At dawn on August 21, a little more than a year after invading the Jackson County seat, Quantrill and 450 raiders entered the sleeping Kansas town. He allegedly ordered his men to "kill every male big enough to carry a gun." They nearly succeeded. Within three hours, the bushwhackers murdered 182 men and boys and burned 185 buildings. Despite being pursued by Union troops, Quantrill and the others returned to Missouri where they scattered and, once again, found sanctuary with confederate sympathizers.

Quantrill's raid shocked the country. For Gen. Thomas Ewing, the commander of the Union army in western Missouri, the Lawrence massacre was the final atrocity. He had grown increasingly frustrated over the guerillas' border attacks.

Four days after the raid, Gen. Ewing issued a decree called Order Number 11. One historian called the infamous order the "harshest military measure directed against civilians during the Civil War."

The order effectively reduced the region to a wasteland. From the Missouri River on the north to the Osage River on the south, the edict depopulated an area 85 miles long and 50 miles wide.

When Gen. Thomas Ewing, shown here, refused to rescind Order Number 11, Missouri artist and pro-Union man, George Caleb Bingham vowed, "If you persist in executing that order, I will make you infamous with the pen and brush as far as I am able." True to his promise, Bingham continued to haunt Ewing even after the retired general moved back to his home in Ohio. Ewing had hoped to achieve distinction as a military leader during the war in order to further his political aspirations. In 1877, when Ewing ran for governor, Bingham exhibited his famous painting, Order Number 11, throughout Ohio. Ewing lost the election, which ended his hopes for a political career. He later confided to a friend that the harsh order changed many lives. "It changed mine, I know," he said. "I sometimes wonder if I had not issued that order . . . what might have happened." Ewing died in 1896 after being hit by a streetcar near his law office in New York City.

Within 15 days of the order's issuance, everyone was forced to leave the region, unless they could prove their loyalty to the Union. People who could not prove loyalty were banished from the district. All their property and any possessions they could not carry were destroyed – or confiscated if useful to the military.

Even the lives of the area's handful of loyalists were disrupted. They were required to live at designated military posts.

The Union's military Post Number One was Blithedale in Hickman Mills. For the remainder of the war, 32 families who passed Gen. Ewing's loyalty test lived at Blithedale. Except for this house, almost all other homes, buildings, supplies and foodstuffs, aside from those that the Union conscripted, were burned or destroyed.

Jacob Palmer, who took the loyalty oath and continued to live on Jefferys' farm, recalled the days soon after the Order: "One day we were threshing rye in a field on the high prairie. We saw fire spring up from a burning building to the Northeast. Before night we had counted seventeen houses in flames all around the circle except in the direction of Kansas City. We thought our time had come but there was no fire in our immediate vicinity."

One Union soldier, also a witness of the devastation, wrote home to his wife, "It is heartsickening to see what I have seen...A desolated country and men and women and children, some of them almost naked. Some on foot and some in old wagons. Oh God."

For many years after the war, this region was called the Burnt District.

By issuing such a punitive order, Gen. Ewing hoped that Quantrill and his men could no longer find sanctuary in Missouri and that rebel raids would cease. But as historian James McPherson pointed out in *Battle Cry of Freedom, The Civil War Era*, "None of this stopped the guerillas... Quite the contrary, their raids became more daring and destructive during the following year."

The Order, like the war itself, divided families and crippled commerce in west central Missouri. It also drove thousands (estimates range from 10,000 to 20,000) of Missourians from their homes. Most of these were left homeless and on the roads, easy pickings for pro-Union highwaymen.

Stephen Slaughter described the effects of the ruinous war on his family: "Most of the people were from the South and favored the South in the war. My father [O.V., a boy during the war]... was sent on errands to give food to Jesse James in his hideouts... My grandfather, Elijah, had two brothers who fought on the side of the North, two on the side of the South.

General Order No. 11

HEADQUARTERS DISTRICT OF THE BORDER

I. All persons living in Jackson, Cass and Bates counties, Missouri, and in part of Vernon included in this district, except those living within one mile of the limits of Independence, Hickman's Mills [sic], Pleasant Hill and Harrisonville, and except those in that part of Kaw township, Jackson county, north of Brush Creek and west of the Big Blue, are hereby ordered to remove from their present places of residence within fifteen days from the date hereof.

Those who, within that time, establish their loyalty to the satisfaction of the commanding officer of the military station nearest their present places of residence, will receive from him certificates stating the fact of their loyalty and the names of the witnesses by whom it can be shown. All who receive such certificates will be permitted to remove to any military station in this district, or to any part of the State of Kansas, except the counties on the eastern border of the State. All others shall remove out of this district. Officers commanding companies and detachments servicing in the counties named, will see that this paragraph is promptly obeyed.

II. All grain and hay in the field or under shelter, in the districts from which the inhabitants are required to remove, within reach of military stations, after the 9th day of September next, will be taken to such stations, and turned over to the proper officers there; and report of the amount so turned over made to District Head Quarters, specifying the names of all loyal owners, and the amount of such produce taken from them. All grain and hay found in such district after the 9th day of September next, not convenient to such stations, will be destroyed.

III. The provisions of General Order No. 10 [issued one week earlier, August 18] from these headquarters will be at once vigorously executed by officers commanding in the parts of the district, and at the stations, not subject to the operation of Paragraph I of this Order – and especially in the towns of Independence, Westport and Kansas City.

IV. Paragraph 3, General Order No. 10, is revoked as to all who have borne arms against the Government in this district since the 20th day of August, 1863.

By order of
Brig. Gen. Ewing
HANNAHS, Adjutant

Many pro-Union people disagreed with Gen. Ewing's Order Number 11. The Missouri artist, George Caleb Bingham, was one. To protest the order, Bingham created the painting shown here: Order Number 11. It shows a family being driven from its home, while Gen. Ewing and his troops look on. Some historians believe that Blithedale, the Jefferys' mansion in Hickman Mills, inspired the house depicted on the left. Bingham said that he had seen men killed while carrying out the order. Among other complaints, Bingham feared that the terrible effects of the order would make reconciliation between district citizens difficult, even after the war ended. Unfortunately, history proved the painter's predictions correct.

Philip Slaughter (Stephen's uncle), a member of the Hickman church, fought on the side of the North." After Order Number 11, Elijah took O.V. and the rest of the family south of Jackson County. Unlike many other families in the Hickman Mills area, the Slaughters returned after the war.

For the first two years of the war, Union forces kept Confederate troops from Jackson County. This was little consolation to citizens living in a county overrun by guerillas on both sides of the conflict. Between 1861-1865 more than 1,100 armed clashes took place in Missouri, and most of those occurred along the volatile western border. The worst border fight, however, occurred between October 21-23, 1864.

Gen. Sterling Price, one time governor of Missouri, had long hoped to capture his state for the Confederacy. In October he began an advance of his Confederate troops toward Jackson County. He planned to pin the Union's army, led by Gen. Samuel Curtis, against the Kaw and Missouri Rivers. The plan failed. Gen. Price and his men advanced no farther than a ridge just south of Brush Creek, near today's Kansas City Plaza. For three days, 30,000 soldiers fought the Battle of Westport, ending in a Confederate retreat.

As Gen. Price and his men fell away from the pursuing Union army, they moved south. Defeated Confederates swept across Washington Township, taking everything they could find that their beleaguered army needed. The Union stubbornly chased them all the way to the Arkansas border.

A little more than five months later, the war ended when Gen. Robert E. Lee formally surrendered to Gen. Ulysses S. Grant at the Appomattox Courthouse, Virginia. Contrary to the military custom of a victorious army, Grant refused to accept Lee's proffered battle sword. Also contrary to custom, Grant allowed all Confederate soldiers to keep their horses.

The blond-haired, blue-eyed, George Todd, shown here, was one of the most brutal of William Quantrill's raiders. Born in Canada, Todd came to Kansas City in 1859 at age twenty and worked with his father who was a stone mason. Father and son built the original Red Bridge at a ford less than one-fourth mile north of today's bridge. The old bridge was of hand-hewn timbers, fastened together with wooden pins, weather-boarded and shingled, and painted red, giving it the name of Red Bridge. Four years younger than Quantrill, George initially idolized the rebel leader, becoming a Second Lieutenant in the guerilla army. By the fall of 1863 when few still believed in Confederate victory, Todd usurped Quantrill's waning control over the border rebels.

Scars of War

Although the Civil War ended with magnanimous gestures in the Appomattox courthouse, its polarizing acrimony remained like a deep canker in west central Missouri. Lost fortunes, lost limbs, destroyed property, destroyed lives – all served as reasons to keep the rancor alive…

…At the close of the war, the government owed Charles Jefferys $20,000, which was never paid. He left the area and settled permanently in Philadelphia. Thirty years later, Jefferys' son, Harry, returned to Hickman Mills to sell the Washington Township property. The family sold the last section in 1905.

…When Edwin Hickman's quest for riches in Colorado failed, he returned to Missouri and joined the Confederate Army. An injury at the battle of Shiloh led to the amputation of his right arm. He wrote his wife, "Kate, I had a tight rub to get well. I had to be fed and could not raise myself in bed for five weeks. The day before my arm was taken off, I lost all appetite and hope." Hope must have returned, however, because he remained with his troops and did not leave the army until the war's end in 1865.

…The Hickman Mills Christian Church, built on land donated by Edwin Hickman, was used as a barracks and horse stable during the war. The war-damaged church did not reopen until 1866.

…After the Highland Academy was burned, Eliza Johnson's sons, Oliver and Will, joined the Confederate Army. Eliza, along with her daughter, Margaret, and the family's slave, fled to Texas. Eliza never returned to Missouri, and her sons died in the war.

"More than any other state," wrote historian James McPherson, "Missouri suffered the horrors of internecine warfare and the resulting hatreds which persisted for decades after Appomattox."

And no other region in Missouri felt those horrors and those persevering hostilities more than Washington Township.

After the issuance of Order Number 11, people were forced to flee on foot over hot, dusty roads, crowded with refugees who had little more than the clothes on their backs or a few household goods they could hastily throw into a wagon. The merciless measures outlined in the order offered an open invitation to highway thugs and revenge-seeking Jayhawkers to assault with impunity unarmed residents fleeing the forbidden zone. Many exiles were robbed and murdered as they fled. Young men were seized from their escaping families and executed by soldiers in charge of supervising the evacuation. The order stipulated the confiscation or destruction of all grain and hay that might fall into the rebels' possession, but fanatical enforcers of the measure, like "Doc" Jennison, a Jawhawker leader, took extraordinary liberties. They burned entire farms. Dotting the landscape throughout rural Jackson County were lone chimneys left amid the charred remains of farmhouses. They were ruefully referred to as "Jennison's Monuments."

Photograph from the U.S. National Archives and Records Administration

Chapter 3: The First Schools

Photograph: Holmes Park School

With every intelligent person I have met, and many others, Missouri has been the subject of conversation. I find all have their minds turned that way. I have no doubt but it will be all the rage in two or three years, just like Ohio was 10 years ago or less. Treasurer of Virginia, 1816.

When Missouri entered the Union in 1821, it ranked 23rd out of 24 states in population. By 1860, on the eve of the Civil War, it ranked 8th.

Although the eastern part of the state developed rapidly in the 1820s, much of the burgeoning population in the 1830s was in Jackson County, especially along the routes of the three great western trails. That profitable corridor, the gateway to the west, was booming. Each year, hopeful, confident residents platted new settlements (most are long-forgotten) near the trails and recorded them as official communities or "townships."

In January 1855, Alexander Chiles and William (Uncle Buck) Muir, whose families had deep roots in western Missouri, recorded a new townsite about two miles east of the Santa Fe and California trails in northeast Washington Township. They called it **Union Point**.

Jefferson Johnson, a leader in the little community, had established Highland Academy there in 1845. A year later, he started Bethlehem Christian Church. (The 13-member church later became Hickman Mills Community Christian Church.) In fact, the strength of Johnson's commitment and leadership probably accounts for the rapid settlement of the area and the founding of Union Point, despite Johnson's death in December 1850.

Photograph courtesy the Jackson County Historical Society, Independence, Missouri.

The family in this photograph – the Hustons from Ohio – were among thousands who came to Missouri during the half century after the territory became a state. Missouri's population was 66,076 in 1820 and 1,182,012 in 1860. Many of the immigrants, like the Hustons, were parents, committed to establishing viable schools for their children.

By 1850 families in Jackson County had created 32 public schools, compared to the entire state of Missouri which had 47 public schools ten years earlier. The longevity of the four original schools in the Hickman Mills C-1 School District is unusual. Many early schools, certainly subscription schools, came and went with little notice. Sometime in the 1850s, for example, between the closing of the Highland Academy and the opening of Union Point School, there was a log school located one-fourth mile west of the Union Point and on the north side of Bannister Road.

The town's original plat, still in existence at Hickman Mills C-1 School District, shows a carefully planned community, near today's Elm Street and Bannister Road. Street names on the old plat include Kansas, High, Independence, Watter and Academy.

Despite all the meticulous plans, however, Union Point failed to grow. Only a school and a blacksmith shop, cater-

Photograph courtesy of the Kansas City Missouri Public Library, Special Collections.

Shortly after the Civil War, when Hickman Mills' leaders applied to the federal government to establish a postal station, a clerk in the Washington D.C. post office department inadvertently changed the spelling of the town's name from Hickman's Mill to Hickman Mills. The erroneous name stuck. By the turn of the century, more than 100 families considered Hickman Mills their hometown.

The town's "residents are imbued with more civic pride than are the citizens of many larger places. [It] has grown from a tiny hamlet...to a town of more than 200 persons. `And we're going to keep right on growing,' says R. D. Barry, cashier of the Hickman Mills Bank...

"Hickman Mills [shown here in the early 1920s] was first established in the dim past. When it gained federal recognition and got a post office it was designated on the postal maps as Jeffries, which name is painted on the railroad station. But the residents clung to the name of Hickman Mills. So Hickman Mills it is...

"Hickman Mills is located at the intersection of the Hillcrest and Red Bridge highways, both of which are paved. It has electric lights, a modern Christian church and adequate education facilities."

From Jackson County, Missouri: Its Opportunities and Resources. Written by M.E. Ballou, published by the Chamber of Commerce, Independence, MO 1926.

cornered from the school, were ever built. In the years to come, young farm boys and men gathered in the field east of the shop for horse and foot races, wrestling matches and shooting contests.

The three overland wagon trails played key roles in the development of the town of **Hickman Mills**. Nevertheless, the town owed its continued growth to the railroads.

Stephen Slaughter wrote, "Transportation into and out of this area in the early 1900s, up to the entry of the auto and the truck, was practically all by train. A man might take four or five or six hogs to Kansas City in a wagon, but it was a long distance and few hogs could be moved at one time."

When Harry Jefferys returned to Jackson County in the early 20th century to sell the family's vast estate, he sold a plot of land near Grandview and Red Bridge Roads to the Frisco Railroad for a stationhouse. The stipulation of the sale was that the station be called Jefferys. The agreement was honored – in a way. Someone got the spelling wrong though. The name on the platform was "Jeffries" and remained that way until the building burned down in 1914. Mail trains continued collecting mail at the Jeffries station until it closed in 1954.

"You bought a ticket to Jeffries," said Stephen Slaughter, "not to Hickman Mills. An attendant, or stationmaster, was there to sell tickets. He had a telegraph machine, which ticked away... Across the tracks from the station were the stockyards or pens, which would hold several hundred hogs and I suppose 50 or so cattle... A pole stood to the south of the station on the west side of the tracks, and a mail pouch was often hung from the pole, and a through train would take the pouch off the pole and the train need not stop."

When ready for market, local farmers drove their livestock through Hickman Mills to the depot.

"[S]everal men, or boys, [ran] ahead to get them on the right road," wrote Slaughter, "and at Jeffries put them in the pens east of the main track. A switch was there for the grain or cattle cars that were needed from time to time. This had to be arranged through the local station agent or by phone to Kansas City. About 70 hogs could be loaded into a hog or cattle car. A man was placed in the car to keep the hogs from piling on each other and so injuring or smothering any on the bottom."

In contrast to the wagon trails' influence on Hickman Mills, the nation's expanding railroad system during the post-Civil War years played a key role in the establishment of **Holmes Park**. A thriving community for more than a half a century, Holmes Park was near today's Bannister Road, between Interstates 71 and 435.

In 1869, the year the transcontinental railroad opened, the first bridge spanning the Missouri River was built in Kansas City. Almost overnight, with the Hannibal Bridge, Jackson County became a hub for railroad transportation. Trains rapidly displaced the covered wagons as the overland transport of choice.

The little town of Holmes Park developed in 1870 when the Blair Line Railroad, running from Kansas City to Clinton, Missouri, was surveyed through the heart of Washington Township. Holmes Park, called Hart Grove during trail days, was named for Robert Holmes, who purchased 640 acres for $1.50 from the government. Holmes and a neighbor then sold the right-of-way to the railroad company.

Stephen Slaughter recalled the area's rail traffic: "The early engines were all steam... [G]asoline engines later began to be added but no electric engines in my time. The steam engines were also enlarged and pulled more cars up

Photograph courtesy of the Kansas City Missouri Public Library, Special Collections.

"In July, 1889, James T. Holmes and Nannie Holmes, his wife, and Patterson Stewart and Mary C. Stewart, his wife, Proprietors of the Town of Holmes Park [shown here] filed a map of the town, which consisted of 7 77/100 of an acre more or less."

During the same month, the four Holmes Park residents "deeded 100 feet right of way to Kansas City & Southern Railway Co...The town plat shows the depot at 4th street and the stockyards north of 3rd street...

"The bluff east of Holmes Park was a rock ledge and when the railroad was being built, B. Lantry & Sons Crushed Stone Co. began quarrying the rock. A large crew was used and close to 30-40 carloads of crushed rock shipped per day to be used for ballast. Some was shipped as far as the Gulf...

"About 1915 a croquet court was built behind the general store. [The two-story general store, built in 1885, is on the left of the photograph.] This became a popular pastime. A team was organized in Hickman Mills and one in Holmes Park."

From "A Panoramic of the Lost Townships," by Mrs. Greenberry Ragan, published by the Jackson County Historical Society, December 1965.

Photograph courtesy of the Kansas City Missouri Public Library, Special Collections.

"About 1900 the Excelsior Powder Manufacturing Company [shown here], manufacturers of blasting powder, built a powder mill at Holmes Park. Several years later, this plant was acquired by the DuPont Company. The DuPont Company ended the business connections with Holmes Park in 1959.

"In 1913 the Outdoor Enterprise Company began the Chinchilla Rabbit Farm in Holmes Park under the management of Edward H. Stahl, a noted fancier of rabbits. The rabbits were raised for both fur and meat and were shipped to many states."

From "A Panoramic of the Lost Townships," by Mrs. Greenberry Ragan, published by the Jackson County Historical Society, December, 1965.

that steep grade from near Holmes Park to more level land to the west of the Hickman grade school. One steam engine, by 1915 or 1920, could pull 70 or more cars up that grade. At times two engines were put on. The Kansas City Southern built the new line through our farm in the 1920s to avoid that grade."

Robert Holmes built a general store in the town at about 96th and Elmwood. During the early 20th century, a black-smith shop operated across the street from the store, and a pool hall was on the southwest corner of 95th and Elmwood. Nearby were two large boarding houses, providing accommodations for the labor force needed in the town's expanding business community.

Easy access to rail lines appealed to several large companies. One, the Excelsior Powder Company, bought property on the southern edge of Holmes Park in 1900. The new plant became the largest powder plant in the midwest, employing more than 100 people. Former residents later recalled that several explosions occurred at the plant through the years, killing a number of workers. Another company, the Outdoor Enterprise Company, ran from 1920 to 1933. It was a large rabbit farm and employed about 75 workers.

Of the four communities important to the development of the Hickman Mills C-1 School District, only one, **Rockford** (some early spellings are Rock Ford), left no record of official colonization. All four communities, however, established the essential element for a frontier settlement: a successful school.

On May 11, 1886, a tornado raged through Jackson County, killing and injuring dozens of people. The storm hit the Hickman Mills area, but the funnel itself cut a swath through Kansas City, ripping the roof off the courthouse. This photograph, taken the next year and the oldest extant photograph of the C-1 school district, shows students at Union Point standing beside the school. The man with the beard was the teacher, Mr. Pulliam. He was credited with saving his students during the storm by insisting that they remain calm and crouch under the long tables that lined two walls.

UNION POINT SCHOOL

1855-1980

The year they registered the Union Point plat, Chiles and Muir allocated a combined 30 acres of their properties for construction of a school. The school's trustees paid $1.00 per acre for the land. Later, when the town failed to grow, Buck Muir reclaimed his 20 acres north of Main Street (Bannister), which left Chiles' 10-acre tract south of the road for the school.

The new frame building was located on the southwest corner of today's Elm Street and Bannister Road and about a mile south of the former Highland Academy. Union Point was the first public school in the area. Prior to Union Point, parents either had to pay for subscription schools or for tutors.

The school year conformed to the agrarian calendar. Vacations occurred during spring plowing and autumn harvesting. While education was important, farm and family obligations took precedence. Former Union Point students had vivid memories of shotguns propped neatly in a corner of the classroom. Older boys often brought their guns to school in order to hunt on their way home.

Like many schools in the region, Union Point closed during the Civil War. Post war years, however, saw a boom in enrollment. By the 1880s, the school was so crowded that one

Daily Record of Union Point School for the Term commencing Sept 7 1896, and ending 18
(Term of School Year.) John H. Hoover Teacher.
No. | PUPILS' NAMES. | Age. | 1st Mo. | 2d Mo. | 3d Mo. | 4th Mo. | Total Days Present. | Total Days Absent. | Times Tardy.
1 Roy Estep
2 Floy "
3 Susie Ervin

Adult commitment to children's education is apparent in every extant document from the district's early schools. Each school had a board of trustees, who maintained careful records, itemizing the cost of everything from teacher salaries to the price of a broom. Teacher gradebooks were equally fastidious, logging attendance (days taught, present, absent, enrolled, tardy and "minutes lost") and evaluating coursework (spelling, reading, writing, arithmetic, grammar, geography, physiology, music and drawing). The right side of the ledger included a generous space for teacher comments. Several pages in the back were set aside for the names of visitors. Shown here is the upper portion of a page from the district's oldest surviving gradebook. It is from Union Point, 1896.

or two older students helped with teaching responsibilities. The regular teacher earned $50 to $60 a month, with an additional $2.50 for janitor work.

The 20th century history of Union Point mirrors that of the other three original grade schools in the Hickman Mills C-1 School District (Rockford, Hickman and Holmes Park). By 1916, 14 years after consolidation of the four schools, the area had grown so rapidly that voters passed a substantial school bond. The money was used for the adoption of free textbooks and for the construction of new brick schools to replace the four original frame buildings. The rebuilt Union Point cost $3,270.

Subsequent major renovations came in 1949 when voters approved a $60,000 bond issue. For the next dozen years, the on-going and rapid increase in the district's student population remained a yearly challenge. It seemed that the district could not build new schools or add new wings fast enough. Gymnasiums, basements, auditoriums were carved into classrooms. Double shifts were initiated – classes starting before dawn and ending at dusk. Finally in the late 1960s and 1970s, the up-swing in enrollment leveled off – and then dropped. By 1980, the last year for Union Point, all four original grade schools had closed.

Holmes Park School

1870s-1979

No one knows the exact year Hart Grove School was built, although some estimates say 1859. Named for the stream that meandered nearby, the school was located on the Santa Fe Trail, not far from the current intersection of Hillcrest and Bannister Roads. Hart Grove functioned as a school for a few years after the Civil War, until it burned.

The school was rebuilt sometime in the 1870s as a one-room, frame structure. This second building was about 50 yards from the brick structure used after 1916 by the consolidated district. Renamed Holmes Park, the school recognized Robert Holmes on whose property the school was built. The initial agreement stipulated that when the school ceased to exist as a learning facility the property would revert to the Holmes family heirs.

The early school educated children from neighboring farms. Later in the 20th century, as the town of Holmes Park grew, the school's enrollment reflected a rise in the number of children whose parents worked in the local factories. Surviving gradebooks and attendance records from the school show a greater turnover in the student population at Holmes Park than is apparent in the books and records from the other three original schools.

Upgraded with $4,684 of the 1916 bonds, the new, brick Holmes Park School was constructed west of the earlier school. During the first half of the century, grades one through eight attended Holmes Park. In 1955, with district-wide enrollment growth, the school housed only primary grades. Five years later, Holmes Park and the other three original grade schools served the district's kindergarten classes. In 1965, 14 years before it closed, 145 first graders attended Holmes Park.

Rockford School

1873-1975

On March 7, 1873, William and Mary Wright, who owned several hundred acres along the Little Blue River in southeast Washington Township, deeded a portion of their land to Aaron Noland and P.C. Smith. The two men were school directors and oversaw the building of a new school, called Rockford. Located at today's Longview and Raytown Roads, the school was built just west of a rocky ledge, a favorite wagon crossing on the shore of the Little Blue River.

With $3,221 of the 1916 bonds, a two-room, brick school was built at the Rockford site. When the district experienced dramatic enrollment increases in the 1950s, the school's small basement was expanded for additional space.

In early 1974, the U.S. Army Corps of Engineers publicized plans to build a reservoir in southeast Washington Township. The proposal called for damming the Little Blue River. Rockford School was within the flood plain of the proposed reservoir, although not within the lake itself. Despite the Corps' plans to purchase the school and land from the district, the agency announced that the historic building might be leased to the district or turned into a museum.

On July 17, 1975, the Board of Education voted to sell the school and the property to the Corps of Engineers for $44,000 for the development of the Longview Reservoir. At that time Rockford was used as a kindergarten for about 100 students who attended school in two shifts. During construction of the lake project, the school was used as an office for the corps staff. The building was razed after the completion of the recreational area.

Hickman School
1890-1980

In 1866, part of the George Hedges farm [see illustration in Chapter 1, page 10] became the site for a school. Named for its benefactor, the small building was situated almost due south of the village of Hickman Mills at today's Highway 71 and 115th Street.

Four years later, J.R. and Wiley Jones, who owned 350 acres about one mile southwest of Hickman Mills, built a school on their property. Jones School, sometimes called the Coon Hollow School, was located near an area later called Kernodle Lake.

Sometime in the early 1890s, the two schools merged. The new, white-framed school, named Hickman School, was constructed at a site between the Hedges and Jones Schools, at the current junction of Grandview and Longview Roads.

The new brick Hickman School was rebuilt in 1916 for $3,190. Through most of its history, until 1953, grades one through eight attended Hickman School. In its final years of operation, the school was used to house the very early grades, and finally to accommodate only kindergarten classes.

Portrait of a School

Stephen Slaughter provides a vivid description of student life in the district's early grade schools. Born in 1901, he attended the first Hickman School and later wrote:

The school accommodated the 50 pupils who attended the school but often the pupils numbered little more than 40. In fact an indoor playroom was put in by building a wall at the east end of the main room and the room still accommodated the pupils. Cloaks were hung in this playroom....

Along the back wall of the school room was a blackboard and a raised platform of about eight inches high on which the teacher's desk was located. The blackboard extended on the sidewalls the length of the platform. Pupils sat in the front seats when they recited, except the first and second graders who stood in the side aisle on the south and the teacher stood near the class. If it was the first grade class, she often stood with the child who was reciting with an arm around the child.

One teacher taught the whole school, always a young woman in my day. She enforced the discipline, she made the rules, a 15-minute recess at 10:30 in the morning, a recess of 15 minutes at 2:30 in the afternoon, one hour for lunch and play at 12:00. School began at 9:00 in the morning and was out, I believe, at 4:00. She was paid $40.00 a month, but it was raised to $50 soon after I started...She used physical punishment with a switch if she thought it was needed, but there were almost no whippings in my day...

I learned my geography in the 3rd and 4th grades, mostly

the 4th. I learned the capitals of every state in the Union. I remember them now. I learned the capitals of Canada and of Europe and of South America. I am not perfect on all of them now, especially the last few years. I learned the important business interests in each city in the U.S. I think we had a course in hygiene and physiology in the 6th grade, and in the 7th grade I learned my grammar. I knew the relationship of every word in a sentence to every other word. I could diagram sentences, give declensions of pronouns, parse the words in a sentence, knew the verbs in all their modes, tenses and their other variations and colors...

Slaughter's description makes one thing perfectly clear: a child graduating from Union Point, Rockford, Hickman or Holmes Park possessed a solid background in the fundamentals.

Many parents, however, dreamed of providing more than a basic education for their children. They wanted something beyond grammar school. Statistically nationwide only one in 10 students, at the end of the 19th century, went to school beyond the age of 14.

The problem facing parents in each of the four schools was complicated. How were they to create and finance a high school for just a handful of grammar school graduates?

Stephen Slaughter wrote, "The old school I attended... had a cistern at the back of the building, filled by rain water from gutters on the roof. Farther to the rear were two outdoor toilets. On the south side of the schoolyard to the rear was a shed for the horses....

"The building itself had high windows on the north and the south, an entrance on the east facing the road, the front of the building narrower than the larger rear section and above this first room was a belfry extending above the main roof. A rope hung down through the ceiling of the front room and a bell was in the belfry. [The bell is now in Hickman Mills Community Christian Church.] This building was pulled across the road [when a new, brick school was constructed in 1916] and placed in the Washer orchard a few feet to the south of its former location and stood there for many years. The small front room and belfry were taken off for the moving..."

The photograph shows the original Hickman School after it was moved to the orchard.

Chapter 4: Consolidation & the Early Years

So many young men waste away their youth in idleness and degrading dissipation when manhood and old age could be so much bettered by more honorable and worthy use… I know that he [Willie] is free from imputations of this kind but I want him to see clearly the rock on which so many split their vessels. Above all I want to see him enter manhood spotless in character and with a cultivated mind. I want him and you, too, to impose the strictest injunctions on Ann Eliza in relation to mental cultivation. Remember that intelligence is acquired more from the careful reading of good books than from any other medium. The simple knowledge of grammar without a subject to converse upon, this is understood, is useless.

One month after losing his arm during the Civil War, Edwin Hickman wrote this in a letter to his wife, Kate, about the education of their children, Willie and Ann Eliza.

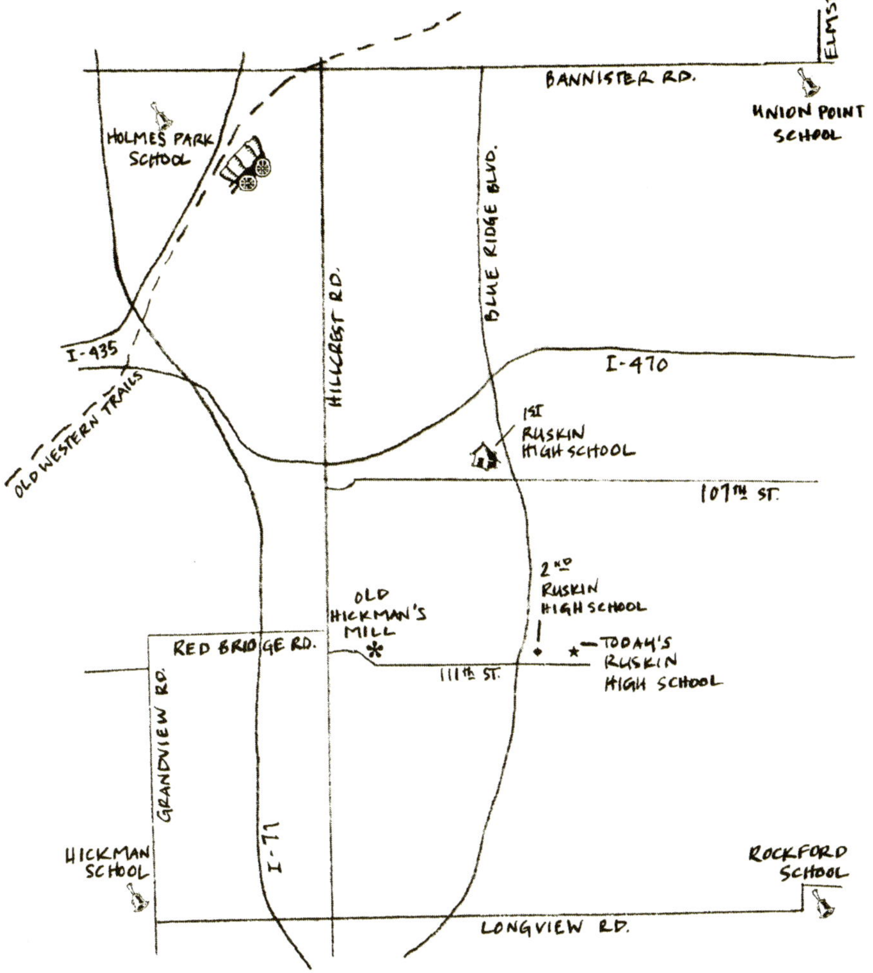

The original grammar schools in Missouri's first consolidated school district represented the geographic four corners of an area in central Washington Township, Jackson County. Rebuilt and upgraded through the years by the district, all four buildings operated as schools throughout the 20th century, but by the year 2000 only two (Union Point and Hickman School) remained standing. At that time, they were owned and operated by two local church communities. For half a century, the district was officially called Consolidated School District No. 1. Only during the latter half of its first centennial was it known as Hickman Mills C-1 School District. Although it was the first district in Missouri to consolidate, i.e. to join grammar schools and a high school under a single governing board, by the 2000/2001 school year, Hickman Mills was one of 451 such Missouri school districts with high schools.

William H. Johnson, shown here in 1897 with his students at Union Point, was born and raised in the Hickman Mills area. An education reformer, Johnson worked tirelessly to bring public high schools to Missouri and was an early, active supporter of the school consolidation law in the state. Eighty-six years after he attended Union Point as a student, 91-year-old Johnson was honored at the school's 100th anniversary in 1955. He lived several more years in Independence before his death.

Thanks to education reformers, publicly financed elementary schools were, in large part, operating nationwide by the start of the 20th century. The battle for public high schools, however, continued. Such schools were rare. Although Boston, Massachusetts, established the nation's first free, publicly supported high school in May 1821, high schools still only existed in a few urban, middleclass areas, with student enrollments based on entrance examinations. Neither the work force nor colleges required a high school diploma. Consequently, fewer than seven percent of 17 year-olds graduated from high school.

But the first forty years of the new century saw the beginning of a sweeping change. From 1890 to 1918, the U.S. built a high school every day, according to David B. Tyack, a Stanford University education historian. Half a million young people attended secondary school in 1900. By 1920, enrollment leaped to 2.4 million. Twenty years later the number again more than doubled to 6.5 million. By that time three quarters of America's children, ages 14 to 17, were in high school, and more than half of the nation's 17-year-olds graduated.

Missouri's first consolidated school district played a leading role in that historic and progressive movement.

O.V. [Orlando Vinton] Slaughter [back row, left] owned a farm near Hickman Mills School. He is shown here with his family, including "the seven good reasons" that inspired him to work so tirelessly to establish a high school in his neighborhood. The consolidation campaign was only one issue that compelled Mr. Slaughter into public service. Along with other community leaders, he helped secure Hickman Mills' place in postal history. On March 15, 1901, the U.S. Post Office launched the rural mail service. The route out of Hickman Mills became one of the first two established in the nation. At its beginning, 128 patrons on the 26-mile route were served.

Photograph courtesy of Nancy Terwilliger and the Slaughter family.

Canvassing And Compromising

Late one night in March 1901, a train pulled into the depot at Jefferson City, Missouri. Two men, O.V. Slaughter and T.T. Moore, who emerged from the train, had traveled 160 miles to the state's capital. Active leaders in their community, Mr. Slaughter was a prosperous farmer in Washington Township, and Mr. Moore owned the general store in Hickman Mills. Another man, William H. Johnson, met them at the train station. Besides attending Union Point as a student in the early 1870s, Willie Johnson also taught at the school (1887-1898) before becoming superintendent of Jackson County Schools (1898-1908).

The next day the three men met with Missouri's General Assembly and explained their reasons for supporting the passage of legislation that would make school consolidation possible. The proposed law allowed two or more common school districts to consolidate into one district and, by the vote of the people, to elect directors and to vote for the necessary bonds to build a high school.

A few days later, on March 21, 1901, the Assembly passed the consolidation measure, which would go into effect in October.

Establishing consolidation as a practical reality, however, was far more complicated. The new education law merely offered official approval. For the law's supporters, the real battle for consolidation had only begun. The next step involved persuasion.

Historians point to a web of economic and social factors to explain the boom in secondary education. From 1890 to 1920, 18 million immigrants poured into the country, and many more Americans abandoned the farms for the nation's increasingly crowded and industrialized cities. Those population shifts provided the concentrated pool of young people needed to sustain large high schools. At the same time, new technologies replaced jobs once held by children, shrinking the labor market for minors. Laws restricting or banning child labor also pushed youngsters out of the workplace, while compulsory-attendance laws pulled them into the schools. Massachusetts enacted the first compulsory-attendance law in 1852. By the turn of the century, 33 states and the District of Columbia had followed, with laws aimed primarily at 8- to 14-year-olds...

It was the Great Depression, however, that gave children a final shove out of the workforce and cemented the idea of high school as a virtual necessity in the minds of Americans. The value of children in the job market plummeted. And they competed with unemployed adults for those jobs for which they remained eligible. In response, many states raised the age of compulsory school attendance from 14 to 16.

From Lessons of a Century: A Nation's Schools Come of Age, by the staff of Education Week, 2000.

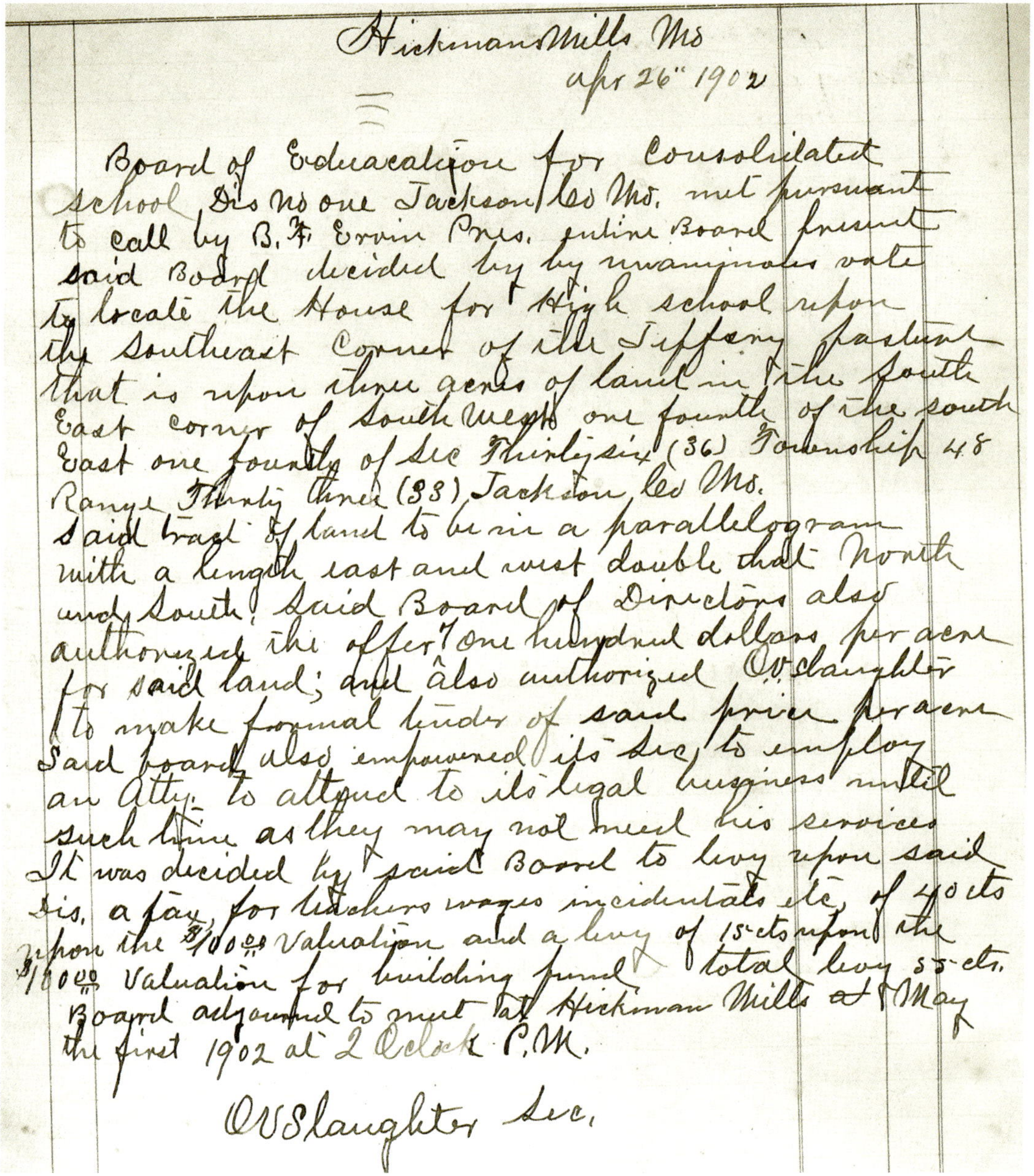

Hickman Mills Mo
apr 26" 1902

Board of Educacation for Consolidated school Dis No one Jackson Co Mo. met pursuant to call by B. F. Ervin Pres. entire Board present said Board decided by by unaminous vote to locate the House for High school upon the Southeast Corner of the Jeffery pasture that is upon three acres of land in the South East corner of South West one fourth of the south East one fourth of Sec Thirty six (36) Township 48 Range Thirty three (33) Jackson Co Mo.
Said tract of land to be in a parallelogram with a length east and west double that North and South. Said Board of Directors also authorized the offer of one hundred dollars per acre for said land; and also authorized O.V. Slaughter to make formal tender of said price per acre Said board also empowered its Sec to employ an Atty to attend to its legal business until such time as they may not need his services It was decided by said Board to levy upon said Dis. a tax for teachers wages incidentals etc of 40 cts upon the $100.00 valuation and a levy of 15 cts upon the $100.00 valuation for building fund total levy 55 cts.
Board adjourned to meet at Hickman Mills at May the first 1902 at 2 Oclock P.M.

O.V. Slaughter Sec.

Minutes from the first C-1 School Board meeting, April 26, 1902:

Hickman Mills Mo
Apr 26th 1902

Board of Education for Consolidated school Dis No one Jackson Co Mo. Met pursuant to call by B. F. Ervin Pres. Entire Board present said Board decided by by [sic] unanimous vote to locate the House for High school upon the Southeast Corner of the Jeffery [sic] pasture that is upon three acres of land in the South East corner of South West one fourth of the south East one fourth of Sec Thirty six (36) Township 48 Range Thirty three (33) Jackson Co Mo. Said tract of land to be in a parallelogram with a length east and west double that North and South. Said Board of Directors also authorized the offer of one hundred dollars per acre for said land; and also authorized O.V. Slaughter to make formal tender of said price per acre. Said board also empowered its Sec to employ an Atty to attend to its legal business until such time as they may not need his services. It was decided by said Board to levy upon said Dis. a tax, for teachers wages incidentals etc, of 40 cts upon the $100.00 valuation and a levy of 15 cts upon the $100.00 valuation for building fund. Total levy 55 cts. Board adjourned to meet at Hickman Mills May the first 1902 at 2 Oclock [sic] P.M.

O.V. Slaughter Sec.

(Like the Slaughter family, the Ervins, for whom today's Ervin Middle School is named, pioneered Washington Township. Their farm was in the Union Point area. After consolidation, the Ervins served on the school board for the next half-century.)

School consolidation was not a new idea. As early as 1897, the National Education Association's committee on rural education recommended a dramatic reorganization of the country's school districts. From that time to 1905, 20 states enacted laws authorizing widely scattered districts to consolidate. Nevertheless, even as late as 1917, the U.S. had an estimated 195,400 school districts – compared to today with fewer than 15,000.

Even before Missouri's legislature acted on March 21, the three men had begun canvassing the neighborhood — the four districts that they hoped to merge into one. For the next year, they traveled around Washington Township urging friends and neighbors to support consolidation. Mr. Slaughter often took one of his seven children along on his visits to the township's constituents. When asked what possible reason he had for spending so much time on the high school issue – after all, he maintained a large farm – Mr. Slaughter said he had seven good reasons. Then he put his hand on the head of the child who'd accompanied him and added, "Here's exhibit A."

In April 1902, the voters of Holmes Park, Union Point, Rockford and Hickman Mills approved consolidation. They also passed a bond issue for $3,250.

That hurdle accomplished, the consolidation advocates faced new obstacles, which involved solutions well beyond a simple yea or nay at the ballot box. To solve these problems required the delicate finesse of a diplomat, the art of compromise.

Rivalry between the four schools had always been fierce. The selection of a single board of directors, which had sovereignty over all the schools, called for district-wide participation. Consequently, the original school board members represented delegates from each school: O.V. Slaughter, B.F. Ervin, W.T. Armstrong, John Hoover, William Snider, and L.W. Holmes.

The location for the high school building also required diplomatic prudence. Picking one school's boundary over another as the site for the new building was not an option. To avoid any turf rivalry, the high school was built at almost the geographic center of the four adjoining grammar schools. Approximately half a mile north of the current Ruskin High School, the site was several yards away from the road, west of today's Blue Ridge Blvd. and north of 107th Street.

Potential pitfalls of selecting leaders and location were resolved. But what about the name for the high school? [In the early years, for the sake of impartiality, the district itself was referred to simply as Consolidated School District No. 1.] For several days the board and voters argued about the new school's name. Holmes Park High School? Hickman High School? McKinley High School? (On September 14, 1901, Pres. William McKinley had died of an assassin's bullet.) When no compromise could be reached, the board asked Willie Johnson to make the final decision. The wise and fair-minded Johnson stayed as far away from politics as possible. He selected the name of the respected British essayist, John Ruskin (1819-1900).

Therefore when we build let us think that we build forever. Let it not be for present delight, nor for present use alone. Let it be such work as our descendants will thank us for and let us think as we lay stone on stone that a time is to come when those stones will be held sound, because our hands have touched them, and that men will say as they look upon the labor and have wrought substance from them, `See, this our father did for us'. John Ruskin, "The Builders."

RUSKIN HIGH SCHOOL

In October 1902, Ruskin High School opened. Total enrollment for Missouri's first consolidated district was 200. Twenty-four (16 girls and eight boys) of those attended the new school. Not since the closing of Highland Academy during the Civil War did the children of central Washington Township have such an opportunity for higher learning. Considering that national census records in 1910 reveal that less than half the population over 25 years old had a grade-school education and only four percent had a college education, this was remarkable for such a small rural community.

In November 1906, Ruskin's student body voted to select the eagle as the official school emblem and blue and gold as the school's colors. Ruskin High School was built on one of the highest ridges in Jackson County, on land formed by glaciers and once owned by Charles Jefferys.

The high school's song acknowledges its unique geographic site:

"Far above the distant landscape
Stands our Ruskin High,
With its walls of strength and beauty
Lifted toward the sky.
Chorus:
Dear old Ruskin, how we love thee,
We will e'er be true
To our colors high above thee,
Gold and Royal Blue.
Symbol of our aspirations
Thou wilt ever be;
Guiding us through life to vict'ry,
Thou shalt keep us free.
(Chorus)

Stephan Slaughter described the uniqueness of the district's early years: "[T]he Hickman Mills community had assumed a stability it had not had 30 years before. We had an established school system, the farms were owned by families that had been in the county for 50 or 60 years, our religious ties were firm, the life of our forefathers was over. We were no longer pioneers, strangers in a strange land."

One room in the high school was furnished and ready for students when the doors opened in October. The school board hired Tilton Young, the high school's one teacher, and equipped the school with a small library. After two years, Dr. Harry Phillips replaced Young, and Alma Aber, an assistant teacher, was hired. The board also furnished the school's second room, purchased laboratory equipment for science classes, and increased the library collection. In 1905/06 teacher salaries in the district totaled $2,680.00.

At the beginning of Ruskin's seventh year, the final debt of the school was paid. A bond-burning celebration was held in Hickman Mills in October 1908.

Originally Ruskin High School offered a three-year program. But as the district's first high school yearbook, *The Mirage*, 1910, pointed out, the goal of the community was to create "an approved first-class high school."

The 1910 *Mirage* explained that to build a curriculum that could one day achieve first-class status, "a third teacher was employed, another room furnished, a larger library bought, better and more laboratory equipment purchased. The school now ranks as second class, has a well designed four-year course of study, three adequately furnished recitation rooms, three teachers, all normal graduates, an enrollment of forty-seven and a term of nine months."

Photographs by Terry Murphy-Latta

These are images of the inside of the Hickman Mills Community Center as it appears today. It is the two-story building on the right in the photograph of downtown Hickman Mills, 1920s (Chapter 3, page 28). The second floor of the center was called Woodman Hall, the location of important events in the area for more than a quarter of a century. The hall, which occupied the entire second floor, had a stage across the north end (top photo). Besides the wide staircase shown in the photograph here (bottom), a separate, smaller staircase allowed guest speakers and performers to enter the back of the stage. The community center hosted the church's holiday celebrations; Ruskin's school dramas and early graduation ceremonies; and political events. In the 1920s it served as a basketball court for Ruskin's athletes during bad weather when the team could not use the outdoor court at the school. During the early years, the downstairs of the building was a general store, with a soda fountain in the front, owned by T.T. Moore. For a while it also housed the town's post office. The building now houses a lawn mower repair shop and the old Woodman Hall is used to warehouse mowers and machine parts.

By the time Missouri's first consolidated school district celebrated its second decade, the world of its founders was rapidly drawing to a close. Several watershed events occurred around that time, prescient warnings of some of the 20th century's most searing social and political turmoils...

...*Birth of a Nation*, D.W. Griffith's pro-Ku Klux Klan film, opened in Los Angeles, California, on February 8, 1915. Eleven months later, the long inactive Klan re-established its charter, granted by the state of Georgia.

...On May 1, 1915, the front page of *The Kansas City Star* announced in bold headlines: "State Faces Huge Deficit." The accompanying article said, "Missouri is broke, worse than broke, for it is believed now that the deficiency in the state's revenue fund will amount to very close to 2 1/2 million dollars by the close of the present year."

...Six days later, in the Irish Sea, a German submarine torpedoed the *Lusitania*, the flagship of Britain's Cunard line. Of its 1,924 passengers, 1,198 were drowned, including 63 babies. American reaction to the 128 Americans who died led to the U.S. entering World War 1.

On the local level, small-town America and the old agrarian life were fading into history. Born in 1901, Stephen Slaughter sensed a profound change: "When I was a boy in the Hickman Mills area our family became aware very early, perhaps by the time I was 12 years old, certainly by the time I was 14 [1915], that this whole region of Jackson County would one day be dominated by Kansas City. Farming would take a back seat. Property values would become much higher, the old life would soon be gone."

This is the first graduating class from Ruskin High School. The 1906 class members were [front row from left] [their later, married names are in brackets] Loraine Morris [Hayworth], Jessie Idol [Blyholder] and Nellie Campbell [Getchell]; [back row] Susie Ervin [Rollins], Margaret Moore, Belle Morris [Hopkins], Luella Campbell [Truman], and Katherine Wells [Whiteley]. Luella's husband, J. Vivian Truman was the brother of Pres. Harry S. Truman. Luella and Vivian Truman's children attended the district's schools and were graduated from Ruskin High School. Katherine Wells' grandfather, Jacob Palmer, farmed the land on which the first Ruskin High School was built. Jessie Blyholder, the class president, and Luella Truman lived to celebrate the district's 75th anniversary in 1977. Jessie's father, Joe Idol, a skilled carpenter in the township, supervised the construction of the 1902 brick and stone high school building.

It wasn't unusual that the graduating class had no boys. In a farm community, such as Washington Township, the boys were needed to work the fields and tend the livestock. In addition, a high school diploma was not required for college admission. One of the boys who left school before graduation was Homer Slaughter. He received an appointment to West Point, where he graduated before leaving for World War I. Two other boys left to attend veterinary college.

The 1907 graduating class included Ruskin High School's first male graduates. Standing, left to right: Georgia Swaney [Pasley], William Slaughter, Helen Holmes [Emery], Lucia Craig [Wintermute], Blanche Whitmore. Sitting, left to right: Alma Johnson [Young], Earl Whiteley, Helen Whitmore

There was no 1908 graduating class. The next year nine seniors [two boys] were graduated.

Stephen Slaughter wrote: "About 1910 or 1912 a basketball court was built to the south of the [high] school building. The boys did the work, the boys paid for everything, mostly from money given by our parents. We bought our own ball for basketball and our own ball for baseball the same way. We bought our own bat for baseball. We had only one. One ball, one bat. Each boy had his own glove for baseball." The players didn't have special uniforms. They wore their school clothes. "The school principal was our coach so far as we had a coach, and he arranged with other schools for games with them. We played Raytown, Lee's Summit, Raymore, Grain Valley, Greenwood, etc." The photographs shown here of the boy and girl basketball teams are from the 1910 Mirage yearbook.

RULES AND REGULATIONS ~ COURSE OF STUDY ~ RUSKIN HIGH SCHOOL

Consolidated District No. 1 ~ Jackson County, Mo. 1911-1912

School Board: B.F. Ervin, President; T.T. Moore, Secretary; L.W. Hones, Treasurer; Z. Hartman, C.S. Campbell, and R.L. Craig.
Faculty: M. MaGee, Principal; Assistants: Miss Katherine Wells and Miss Mary Sue Hopkins.

I. Purpose
It is the desire of the School Board to place this school on a firm basis and equal standing with the best high schools in the state. In order to do this we wish to establish a permanent course of study and give to every patron a general idea of the work and scope of the school. We earnestly hope that each will cooperate with us and the faculty in making ours the best high school possible. *School Board.*

II. Course of Study
The course of study has been arranged to meet both the needs of the school and also the requirements of the State Board of Education for the first class high school.

Freshman	**Credit**
Physical Geography	1 point
Algebra	1 point
Rhetoric	1 point
Ancient History	1 point
Sophomore	
First year Latin	1 point
American Literature	1 point
Algebra	1 point
Medieval and Modern History	1 point
Junior	
English Literature	1 point
Plane Geometry	1 point
Caesar	1 point
Botany	1/2 point
English History	1/2 point
Senior	
English Classics	1 point
Physics	1 point
American History and Government	1 point
Solid Geometry	1/2 point
Higher Arithmetic	1/2 point

Note: One half year in agriculture has been dropped and added to eighth grade.

Brief Outline of Work Offered in Each Course.

MATHEMATICS

Algebra — First Year
Well's *Algebra for Secondary Schools* is the text used. The fundamental processes will be mastered, work to extend well into the study of simultaneous equations, emphasizing functional ideas of equations and use of graphical representation.

Second Year
Same text as first year. Continuation of first year's work dealing with theory of exponents quadractrics, binomial theorem progressions, etc. Special attention given to practical problems and use of graphs.

Plane Geometry
Lyman's *Geometry* is text used. Emphasis placed on practical applications of geometry. Special attention given to form and clearness of proof. Correlation of Algebra with Geometry carefully noted.

Solid Geometry
Same text as plane. Much of the work in this half year will be taken in solving exercises. Special study of measurements will be emphasized.

Higher Arithmetic
Second half of Senior year in mathematics given to study of practical problems of business and commercial arithmetic. Work based on Smith's text.

ENGLISH

First Year — *Rhetoric*
Herrick & Damon text used.
Emphasis on study of words, figures of speech, construction as applied to sentences and paragraphs, and principles of composition.
Study of at least two classics.
Original composition work and reports on outside reading required.

Second Year
Text to be selected. The work in American Literature will consist of the study of biographies of our greatest authors, a study of the history of the growth of our literature and a study of several classics. The style, form and tendencies of each period will be carefully noted.

Third Year
Halleck's *History of English Literature*.
A historic review of English literature and periods, with a study of such classics as Chaucer's Prologue to *Canterbury Tales*, *L'Allegro*, *Il Penseroso*, *Comus*, Cotter's *Saturday Night*, and *Prisoner of Chillon*, *Macbeth* and one other drama from Shakespeare.
Note books required.

Fourth Year
Study of all classics required for college entrance, which have not been included in the first three years' work. All candidates for graduation required to prepare satisfactory theme [original] of not less than fifteen hundred words.

HISTORY

Ancient History

Myers text is used. This year's work will cover a short study of China, India, Egypt, Assyria, Babylon, Phoenicia, Persia and the Hebrews. Their religion, education and social conditions will be compared and their contributions to the world's civilization carefully noted. As thorough a study of Greece and Rome as time and opportunities permit. Note book and special papers from reference reading required.

Medieval and Modern History

Myers text. Papers required on special topics, such as Rise of Papacy, Crusades, Mohammedanism, Feudalism, Reformation, etc. Note book work a requirement.

English History

Montgomery's text. This half year's work will consist mostly of a study of the rise of democracy and special attention will be given to the changes in English government and the growth of constitutional rights.

American History and Government

Channing's *American History* and Hinsdale's *American Government* are texts used. Special emphasis placed upon growth of parties and political ideals, foreign relations, slavery question and the general development of the nation. Civics is taken up when questions of constitutional history arise. Note book work on reference reading required.

SCIENCE

Physical Geography

The work in this course will consist of class and laboratory work based upon Dryer's *Lessons in Physical Geography*. A careful study will be made of the earth as a planet, the surface of the earth, discussion of land and sea forms, movements and transitions. Special attention will be given to atmospheric conditions, plant and animal life in relation to man.

Botany

Text: Coulter's *Textbook of Botany*. The work in this course will consist of a general study of seeds, seedlings, roots, stems and leaves. Laboratory work will be given to study flowers, fruits, pollination and seed development. A study of the great class of plants will be given, covering the algae, fungi, mosses, firs, conifers and flowering plants. The work will be concluded with a brief study of association of plants and general classification. Note books required.

Physics

Hoadley text. The work in this course will consist of a study of the principles of forces of gravity and mechanics of matter, the theories and laws of sound and light. The course will be concluded with an elementary study of electricity. Two hours laboratory work per week will be given. Note books required.

LATIN

First Year

Text: Collier and Daniell's *First Year Latin*. Emphasis and special drill is given to rules and principles of English and Latin grammar, inflection of parts of speech, building of vocabulary and oral translations.

Caesar

Four Books of Caesar will be read. The work will consist of oral reading and sight translation. Much emphasis will be placed on construction work.

Text: (Gunnison and Harley)

III. RULES CONCERNING GRADING AND STANDING

1. Before a pupil can be enrolled in regular class he must be classified by faculty.
2. No pupil will be admitted to any grade who cannot show proper grades and standing entitling him to that grade.
3. Pupils must take regular course. No pupil can take less than four subjects or more without teacher's consent.
4. Pupils failing for two consecutive school months on fifty per cent of their work will be transferred to a grade lower or dismissed from school.
5. The average grade necessary for promotion is 75. A pupil making a grade below 75 in any subject fails in that subject.
6. Those whom the faculty report unfavorably as not having completed the prescribed course will not be graduated.
7. Those entering the ninth grade must show county certificates of graduation from eighth grade or its equivalent.
8. Those who are absent for more than fifteen days in one semester are not entitled to grades for that semester.

IV. GENERAL RULES OF DISCIPLINE

A pupil may be expelled for:

1. Open rebellion.
2. Continual disobedience to rules.
3. Carrying or using tobacco on school ground.
4. Use of profane language on school ground.
5. Refusal to do work required.
6. Destroying or marring school property.

MISCELLANEOUS

1. Tuition of $2.00 per school month in advance.
2. Report cards will be given to each pupil at the close of each month. The parents are urged to examine these cards.
3. Teachers will be furnished with ledgers in which they will keep accurate record of grades and attendance of every pupil enrolling.

In 1916, Harry S. Truman was elected to the school board of Consolidated School District No. 1 to fill a vacancy. He left this position to join the army during World War I. He visited the district's Community Center in 1922 when he campaigned for clerk of Jackson County, his first political office.

Stephen Slaughter told this story about Truman: "Harry was in our house [in Hickman Mills] a number of times that I remember. He was the family representative that came down when mutual problems arose over fences or any subject that required discussion. Only once did he come as part of the Truman threshing crew in exchange of work... In 1919 and the war over, Harry was home for a few weeks before he and Bess were married. There was a sudden rash of hog cholera in the neighborhood, and we had 40 or so young shoats to vaccinate. On a Saturday night Father [O.V. Slaughter] phoned the Trumans. Matt answered the phone, and said she would send someone down early the next morning to help out. Father was not able to do that kind of work, and it left only the hired man and me to help Ed Young, the veterinarian. The next morning at sunrise Harry rode his horse into the barn lot, and we started to work.

"We were not surprised that it was Harry who came. It was the natural response of a neighbor, but he had only recently come home from the war, and he had been asked to appear at many functions. Only a few days before he had made a talk at the Ruskin High School alumni meeting.

"It was the last work he did on the farm. The next week he and Bess were married at his home [sic] in Independence."

Truman's wedding photograph is at the left.

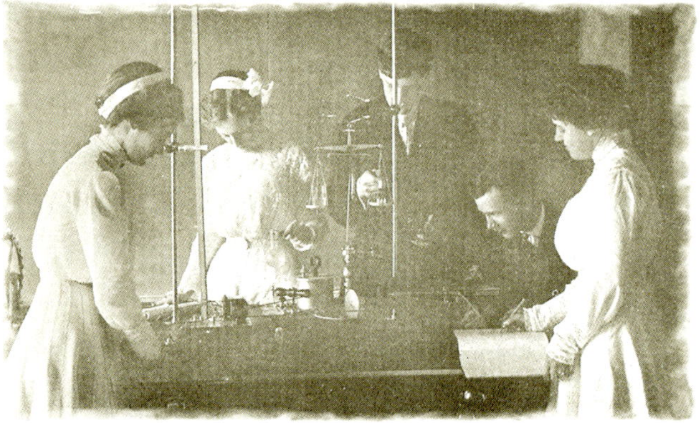

Major world events conspired to thwart the district's early goal of attaining first-class status for its high school. World war and a global economic depression drained manpower and money. By the time the second high school building was complete, in 1931, Ruskin would be a "fully accredited first class high school," according to the 1929 Mirage. The 1910 Mirage, the last yearbook published until 1929, featured these two photographs. The top one shows the agriculture class learning how to "score" a cow. The bottom photograph shows the high school laboratory.

Photograph courtesy of the Harry S. Truman Library, Independence, Missouri.

Chapter 5: Mid-Century Growth

Photograph: The second Ruskin High School, built in 1931, was later used as a junior high school and destroyed in the 1957 tornado.

Signs of "the old life" passing into history were everywhere.

In 1905, the end of an era occurred when Harry Jefferys, son of Charles Jefferys, sold the family's last piece of property in Washington Township. The only remaining tie to this pre-Civil War family was severed when Harry, the last Jefferys to live in Jackson County, Missouri, returned in 1910 to Philadelphia, the family's home.

Jefferys' vast land holdings were parceled out into single-family farms around the village of Hickman Mills. Some became small residential plots.

At the turn of the century, Jackson County's urban areas increasingly encroached onto the neighboring countryside. In 1907, for example, a hopeful young real estate developer named J.C. Nichols bought 10 acres of swamp-land along Brush Creek, just south of Westport, a historic settlement already annexed to Kansas City in 1897. The next year, 1908, when Henry Ford introduced the first Model T, America's urban propulsion into the shrinking countryside commenced in earnest.

Keenly aware of the rural-to-urban metamorphosis in the still largely bucolic Washington Township, Stephen Slaughter wrote, "By 1920, or a few years before, we had stopped growing wheat, a standard farm money crop. Why? Because other farmers had stopped growing it. It was impossible to find neighbors with whom we could swap work to do the threshing...Many new names were in the county. Many remained a few years and left. The county and local community were changing. I knew the newcomers, many of them came to

Ruskin

High School

This Certifies that

Minor M. Slaughter

...ing completed the Course of Study prescribed by the Board of Education, is hereby declared a Graduate of the Ruskin High School, and as an Honorable Testimonial of the Excellence of his Character and Scholarship, is entitled to this

Diploma

Consolidated Dist. No. 59, Jackson County, Missouri, this ____ day of ____, A. D., 191_

Superintendent — President, Secretary — Board of Directors

Minor Slaughter, one of O.V. Slaughter's children, received this diploma, which measures 20 inches by 16 inches, in 1915. Shortly after graduation he joined the army, like thousands of young men, and went to fight in World War I. Stationed in France, Minor survived the war, but died of tuberculosis a few years later. His brother Stephen later wrote, "World War I was an important event in our lives and every family was affected. There was some comment as to how the German families in the Union Point community, those of German ancestry, might react, but I am sure the talk was without foundation. I had four brothers in or involved in the war, one brother Homer, a West Point graduate and his life spent in the army, was in Russia most of the time and was at Ekaterinburg the day after the Czar was murdered...A number of young men and boys in the community were involved in one way or another in the war. Actually it was the flu epidemic that brought the local casualties."

In the last year of the war (1918), the nation was in the grip of a Spanish influenza epidemic. Responding to the "grippe," as it was popularly called, The Kansas City Star frequently offered various remedies from local physicians and health authorities. According to many experts, the appearance of the illness was largely blamed on rampant kissing.

Photograph and diploma courtesy of Nancy Terwilliger and the Slaughter family.

Photograph courtesy of the Kansas City, Missouri, Public Library, Special Collections.

The national Automobile Club started on October 16, 1900, the same year that 8,000 cars were registered in the U.S., which at that time had only 10 miles of paved roads. This is compared to 18 million horses and mules then used for transportation. Cars were a luxury item for the wealthy. (The 1926 photograph shown here is the Kansas City Automobile Club, which before being destroyed by fire, was near the intersection of today's Grandview and Red Bridge Roads in Hickman Mills.)

After World War I, however, many Americans went on a buying spree. Top of the list of popular items was the automobile. Fueling consumer enthusiasm was a drop in Ford automobile prices, which hit their lowest level in 1924 at $290. (In 1909, the price for a Model T was $950.) On June 15, 1924, Ford Motor Company announced the production of its 10 millionth car. It had taken seven years for the company to build its first million cars, but only 132 days in 1924 to reach the ten million mark.

Although Hickman Mills had the second oldest rural mail route in the country, mail carriers still used a horse-drawn cart even after automobiles were in fairly common use. The roads in Washington Township were not all paved, and rain or snow made many roads impassable, even into the early 1930s.

church and entered the church-community life, but to me, an old-timer, the change was drastic. When I left for Drake University the fall of 1921 (I had been at home one year after high school), the turnover had made great headway; when I graduated in 1925 and left for Columbia University in New York City that fall, the turnover was, to me, almost complete. The old life was gone and if the new life had not taken over, it was well underway. The future was plain. So while to you [outsiders] we were still a rural community, to me we were well on our way to the new."

In 1921, with T.T. Moore as president, the Hickman Mills Bank opened across the street from Woodman Hall. The next year, electricity became Hickman Mills' first public utility. The town's second utility, gas, followed two years later.

In the early 1930s, Jackson County voters approved a capital improvement project that allowed for the expansion of Blue Ridge Blvd. from Independence to Grandview. The road construction facilitated the growth of the Hickman Mills school district, which was bisected by the boulevard. One of the key supporters of the issue was the county's presiding judge, Harry S. Truman, who had deep roots in the community.

Increased automobile traffic also spurred federal road improvements. Missouri Highway 1, once a dirt road, then gravel and later called U.S. Highway 71, was paved in 1927. During that same year, Henry Ford's automobile plant produced its 15-millionth Model T.

Responding to population growth, the school board of Missouri's Consolidated District No. 1 sought funding to upgrade the school buildings. Strong, if not widespread, resistance followed. A vocal contingency of anti-tax residents argued that school consolidation had proven financially inefficient. They wanted to return to the neighborhood – or one-school district – system. In 1914, the issue reached the ballot box. On the annual Election Day, residents voted whether to dismantle the state's first consolidated school district. The results were decisive: 44 voted for dismantling and 139 against.

Two years later, with renewed commitment to their consolidated schools, voters approved more than $15,000 in bonds to replace the district's four original frame schools with large brick buildings.

In 1908, Consolidated School District #1 added a third room to the original Ruskin High School and a third teacher joined the staff. Sixteen years later a fourth teacher was hired. A steady rise in enrollment, however, necessitated adding two more teachers just four years later.

Lamenting the reluctance of voters to support plans for a new and larger second high school building, which architects had already designed, the student editors of the 1928/29 Mirage wrote:

"What is that which hangs wavering on the horizon? Truly it is a mirage – an intangible object which evades the blind gropings of an entire community. It is a beautiful dream with which to fill our spare moments. Can it never become a reality? Must we always have our dream turn into a nightmare on election days?

"It is a vital problem, one which must be settled for once and for all in the near future. The world over, it is known that good schools and prosperity go hand-in-hand. It is in the schools that the future citizens are trained, those who must pilot this great nation of ours in the decades to come. Therefore, is it not important to give them every possible advantage while they are in the formative period?

"This new building would give Ruskin one of the best high schools in the State. In planning it, the conditions of other high schools were studied, their good points adopted and their defects eliminated. The result has been a model building which would be equipped for vocational courses as well as for the required courses which are now taught exclusively. This building would also be an imposing structure to which anyone could point with pride as his High School.

"Therefore, it would seem that something should be done to remedy this long-neglected situation that has been such a blot on the community."

Shortly after the yearbook went to press, district voters finally approved bonds for a second Ruskin – which soon became "one of the best high schools in the State."

[The second Ruskin High School is shown above and also on the first page of this chapter.]

The centrally located gymnasium/auditorium in the second Ruskin High School is shown in these three photographs. Everyone who visited the building remembered that big space – the largest school gymnasium in the region at the time it was built.

The 1937 Mirage proudly reported: "In 1931 the beautiful school building… was completed and the staff of six teachers now teach: English, Home Economics, Commerce, Mathematics, History and Science. Thus the school of one room and one teacher has progressed to its present high standing as a fully accredited first class high school."

Nineteen years later, in February 1950, mid-century growth forced voters to approve a $72,000 bond issue for an annex for Ruskin High School.

Photographs courtesy of Bill Ward

A New High School With a Platoon

Not surprisingly Ruskin High School faced the same growing pains as the original grade schools. When Ruskin first opened in 1902, 24 students enrolled in the high school. The entire district at that time, all five schools, had approximately 200 students. Within the next generation, enrollment quadrupled. In 1923, Ruskin had more than 100 pupils. The increased enrollment was due in part to the district's acceptance of tuition-paying students from the districts of Center, Martin City and Dallas, a community near today's Watts Mill.

By 1900, like 33 other states, Missouri had a compulsory-attendance law for children of elementary-school age. High school enrollment was augmented from such mandates at the grade school level. In 1900, 6.4 percent of all 17 year olds in the U.S. graduated from high school. Ten years later the percentage rose to 8.8. By 1920, however, the number almost doubled with 16.8 percent of 17 year olds finishing high school. Rates continued to rise for the next 70 years.

In response to the overcrowding at Ruskin High School in the early 1920s, the board once again sought increased funding. They hoped to build a new high school, three times larger than the 1902 school. This time voter resistance prevailed. Several times since the 1916 bond election, district residents had been asked for additional money. In 1923, a proposition for a 20-cent levy increase on each $100 valuation (making a total levy of 60 cents on each $100) was put on the ballot. The money was targeted for additions to Hickman, Rockford and Union Point Schools and for hiring two teachers for each building. The levy lost. A month later, a special election was held for a $17,000 bond issue, aimed exclusively for the building additions. This time the proposition passed with 124 for and 10 against.

Photograph courtesy of the U.S. National Archives and Records Administration

In 1946, the school board asked R.W. Harmon, who worked as a janitor for the Consolidated #1 School District, if he would like to help transport students. At that time, Mr. Harmon would later recall, the district also contracted with "a widow woman." The woman, named Evelyn Hopkins, drove children in her privately owned bus. A single bus, however, was not enough with increased enrollment after the war.

Harmon, who welcomed the extra income, went to four banks before he found one willing to loan him the money to buy a used bus. For the next year or so, Harmon worked as janitor during the day and drove his bus in the morning and afternoon.

One day, Mrs. Hopkins asked Harmon if he would like to buy her bus and take over her contract with the district. A deal was soon struck.

Years later, Harmon, who built the Harmon Bus Company into the second largest in the nation, liked to point out that he doubled his inventory and profits in a single afternoon.

Harmon's sons, Bob and Dick, both Ruskin High School graduates, eventually took over the business in 1957. Long-time community activists, the brothers sponsored year-round athletic programs for school children in the area.

When the family-owned business was sold to Mayflower Corp. in 1984, it was generating $70 million in annual revenues.

With the first hurdle successfully cleared, the board again went to the voters for the money to build a large new high school. Voters refused. Three times the bond issue appeared on the ballot, and three times it failed. Finally on the fourth try, in late 1928, district residents approved money for a third Ruskin. Harvey Kemper, a district resident at the time, recalled that interest in the hotly contested issue brought out every eligible voter.

About a half mile south of the first school, a 10-acre site was selected for the new high school. The land, originally part of the Jeffreys farm, cost $6,500. (Twenty-four years later (1952), when the board purchased 25 additional acres for the campus, the cost was $14,655.) Condemnation proceedings delayed construction for almost three years.

Finally in 1931, the high school was finished. With a price tag of $84,500, the two-story brick building had 10 classrooms, which, along with the administrative offices, were built around a centrally located gymnasium and auditorium. For the next several years, because the impressive new gym was the largest in the Kansas City area, Ruskin served as host to the Midwest Conference games. Besides the large court, the gym had six-row bleachers on the north and south sides and a stage floor on the east end. The Independence radio station, KIMO, broadcast all conference games, which were announced by local newscaster, Harold Ensley.

Ruskin's large central space served as the village town square. Events once held at Woodman Hall now took place at the school. Holiday programs, plays and musicals, debates, chorale ensembles, 8th and 12th grade graduations, student fairs and PTA fundraisers, professional shows by visiting theatrical performers – the district's showplace served them all.

The design of the second Ruskin High School was inspired by the nationally popular "platoon" system, also called the work-study-play program. The system, developed by educational reformer, John Dewey, reached its zenith during the 1920s. Dewey's idea was "All learning is transmitted through speaking and writing," and a centrally located gym/auditorium offered a hub, according to Dewey, for education's four important academic elements: speaking, listening, music and the arts.

As the focal point for Dewey's four-element system, the gym/auditorium provided space for a wide range of academic and social activities throughout the day, and often at night. Every student spent at least one hour a day in the auditorium. Students gave speeches, sang, and performed plays. They questioned and reviewed each other's presentations. Small groups received special instructions on diction, speech and music appreciation. In classrooms built around the large room, students learned math, science, home economics and other subjects. At night the room often became a community center, used to show popular films or to stage community theater.

No sooner was the second Ruskin High School built than the district experienced a brief period of declining enrollment. The decline was sudden, and its cause arose from an event that occurred 1,500 miles away.

THE DEPRESSION YEARS

On October 29, 1929, called Black Tuesday, a record 16,410,030 shares were traded on the stock exchange, with enormous blocks of stock being dumped for whatever they would bring. By December 1, stocks on the New York Stock Exchange plummeted in value by $25 billion. During the next two years, approximately 11,000 banks – 44 percent of the nation's financial institutions – failed. In 1931, the government reported that four to five million Americans were out of work.

When the new Ruskin High School opened in the fall of 1931, approximately 100 students enrolled. The total enrollment district-wide was about 260, a reduction from the past year and a direct result of economic depression and rising unemployment. During the first year of the new school, national wages were 60 percent less than in 1929. National statistics released in 1933 bore out the local impact on schools: 200,000 of the nation's certified teachers were unemployed, and an estimated 2,280,000 children were not attending school.

In the first part of the 20th century, 80 percent of financing for the nation's schools came from local support. By 1933 that changed. The Depression made shambles of district budgets. In response, states stepped in to shoulder the burden. In the 1930s, state money to schools increased from 17.3 percent of the total to 29.2 percent. The percentage rose to 39.8 in 1950. Today state support to schools, K-12, represents, on average, the majority of a district's budget.

In response to the grim economic news after 1929, a teacher in Consolidated District No. 1 decided to organize a parent/teacher group. Fay Higgins (later Fay Zenor) hoped to pool scarce resources and to purchase supplemental materials and equipment for classrooms. Beyond the basic necessi-

Photograph courtesy of J.B. Brown

The Pennington Chicken Dinner Farm, shown here in about 1948, was a popular restaurant on Hillcrest Road near 109th Street from 1915 to 1961. Maggie Pennington, a widow who started the business, also took in boarders. Through the years, teachers and other staff at the district lived at the boarding house. J.B. Brown, a nephew of Mrs. Pennington, attended district schools and worked at the Farm. He remembers that the home-style restaurant attracted well-known clientele, including Pres. Truman and his family and many popular entertainers of the time, such as Ginger Rogers, Penny Singleton, and Craig Stevens.

By mid-century, with the rapid population growth, Hickman Mills was a popular place to do business. Sam Walton, the 20th century's most prosperous retailer, started his business in the early 1950s with several five-and-ten-cent stores in Arkansas. In 1954, seeing the potential of retail chains in the suburbs, Walton opened his first store in a shopping center at Hickman Mills' new Ruskin Heights, which had opened the year before.

Local business leaders and parents, actively involved in community service, have played key roles in strengthening the school district throughout its 100-year history. The district owed its founding and early growth to deeply committed business leaders. In 1947 Hickman Mills School District's PTA sponsored a new program, the Child Health Clinic, which provided medical assistance and immunizations for many children in the area. In the early 1950s, to foster school spirit, the local Chamber of Commerce and the Lions Club held a free pig roast at the first football game of the season.

ties of keeping coal in the buildings' furnaces and meeting payroll, the district's budget could not be stretched to include ancillary items. On September 18, 1931, the Hickman Mills School Association of Parents held its first meeting. Shortly afterwards, the 44-member group presented the district with a victrola and a radio. Two years later, the parents association raised money to install telephones in each school and to launch an immunization program.

Although parents helped defray some expenses, the school board was forced to initiate a belt-tightening policy. For the 1933-1934 school year, district leaders levied a $4.00 monthly charge for each out-of-district pupil. Teachers' salaries were reduced 10 percent for the coming year, which meant that teachers – two each at Rockford, Hickman, Holmes Park and Union Point – would earn $80 a month. (Salaries were slightly higher for Ruskin's five teachers, with one designated as principal.)

C.A. Burke Elementary School, shown below, was built a few blocks west of Ruskin High School and featured a new design for schools called "finger construction," because its wings spread out from a central hallway. Overcrowding in the district became so acute that during Burke's second year its multipurpose room was partitioned into four classrooms, and the stage was used as a fifth. This emergency arrangement meant that lunch was served in the hallways. Ben Ervin, whose family members were early settlers in Washington Township and were C-1 district board members for several generations, remembered that his father helped build the stone wall around Burke's trash barrels. The stone was from the wall surrounding the old Charles Jefferys farm.

C.A. Burke, who lived with his family for many years in the house just west of Woodman Hall in Hickman Mills, was the district superintendent for 20 years, 1923-1943. This photograph appeared in the 1937 Mirage, along with the caption: "Superintendent C.A. Burke, affectionately known as "Prof", holds a place in the hearts of all Ruskin students. Although we sometimes try his patience to the extent that he has to lecture us, it is soon over and forgotten by all. He has tried to lead and help us through our high school days and the advice he has given us, though not always heeded, has left a lasting impression in our heart [sic] and minds."

Within 100 days of taking office on November 8, 1932, Pres. Franklin D. Roosevelt and his administration used unprecedented powers to launch a series of sweeping social and economic programs designed to lift the nation out of the depression.

The relief programs faced a setback in 1934. Record-breaking freezes in February, and a stubborn heat wave in July, precipitating the worst drought in midwest history, brought devastation to farmers.

Yet despite this bad news, 1934 saw unemployment drop by more than four million and the purchasing power of workers rise by 25 percent nationwide. That year only 58 banks failed. (The annual average since 1921 had been 901.)

The residents of Hickman Mills felt the tangible benefits of the Roosevelt programs. In 1936, for example, through an enabling law (Public Utilities Act of 1935), a public utility providing water was installed in the Hickman Mills area, making the town the third community in the state to receive such service.

Although legislative actions helped solve many of the nation's economic woes, financial recovery was largely due to an increase in orders for military supplies that flooded the nation's factories during the late 1930s. While the U.S. struggled with the Depression, tensions in Europe mounted when Germany's Adolf Hitler invaded Austria and Czechoslovakia. The Nazi leader then focused his attention on Poland, finally invading that country on September 1, 1939.

Two days after Germany invaded Poland, Great Britain and France, the chief buyers for U.S. military goods, declared war on Germany. Maintaining a long-established isolationist policy, the U.S. announced its neutrality.

Staying on the Sidelines Proved Difficult

On the day England and France went to war, 30 Americans died when a German submarine sank the British passenger liner, *Athenia*. United States neutrality also held when, on October 17, 1941, a German submarine torpedoed and damaged the U.S. destroyer *Kearny* off the coast of Iceland, and again 13 days later when the Germans torpedoed and sank another destroyer, the *Reuben James*, near Iceland. But even the deaths of 100 *Reuben James* sailors did not shake the nation's official nonalignment policy.

All that changed, however, on Sunday, December 7, 1941. Shortly after 7 a.m., Japanese warplanes attacked U.S. naval ships at Pearl Harbor, Hawaii. The next day the U.S. declared war on Japan.

Hearing the news, several Ruskin High School students walked out of classes early. That afternoon they enlisted in the nation's military forces.

THE WAR COMES HOME

Marjorie Langford, who taught and worked as a counselor in the district from 1943 to 1981, remembered the war years. "Bendix [at the time called Pratt-Whitney] was the nearby war plant. Both women and men worked there. That was one of the reasons it was hard to get qualified teachers in those days. One of the women teachers at Ruskin, for example, served as the bandleader. Now that's not odd today, but back then it was highly unusual. School buses stopped running, and food was rationed in the schools. We had lots of bean dishes and hardly any sugar."

Rationing was a way of life during the war years. Americans received ration stamps to buy all the basics, including sugar, gasoline, coffee, meat, fat, canned goods, cheese and shoes.

Attendance at parent/teacher association meetings in the district dropped. With so many local men fighting overseas, mothers and other women worked in war factories like Pratt-Whitney. Rummage sales provided funds for many PTA projects, but even those efforts were hampered due to government-sponsored recycling drives for rubber, paper and metal. Nearby Watts Mill on Indian Creek (near 103rd and State Line Road) was stripped of its nine tons of ironwork and then donated to the government to help in the scrap iron drive.

In May, 1944, U.S. Sen. Harry S. Truman spoke to an assembly at Ruskin High School. A former district board member, the Missouri politican had dozens of close friends in Hickman Mills. His brother was J. Vivian who married Luella Campbell, a member of Ruskin's first graduating class. Three of the couple's five children graduated from Ruskin between 1937 and 1944. Promising victory against America's enemies, the Senator reassured Ruskin students and other guests that "the world offers a bright future to young people."

A month later, on June 6, Allied Forces invaded Normandy. Nominated and elected that fall for U.S. Vice President, Truman was in office less than three months when the sudden death of Pres. Roosevelt catapulted him to the presidency. Barely a month later, Germany surrendered and by the end of the summer Japan did likewise.

"You didn't know whether to laugh or cry," remembered Marge Langford, whose brother was killed in the war. "And so you did both. It was over. Everyone celebrated. Hickman Mills Community Church – the biggest church in the area at that time – held an end-of-the-war service. The sanctuary was overflowing. Very emotional service. Later I went downtown to Union Station. There was a massive rally there. What a crowd! What a celebration!"

THE BABY BOOM YEARS

In the months following the war's end, soldiers and sailors returned home, and communities across the nation experienced a critical demand for new housing. Post-war brought on an explosion in real estate development, especially on the outskirts of large cities. Many farming communities were soon divided – and subdivided – into a phenomenon known as the suburbs.

Ancillary to the suburban growth was a population upturn – the baby boom – that began in 1946 and lasted until 1964. The year when Kansas City celebrated its 100th anniversary, 1950, *The Kansas City Star* reported, "The greatest population surge in the history of the Metropolitan Kansas City – indicating about 800,000 persons now live in the area – has been recorded within the last decade." Jackson County, which included Hickman Mills, represented more than 460,000 of that number.

The old village certainly experienced the "population surge." In the year of *The Star* article, Hickman Mills had 2,500 residents. Nine years later the number was 23,000 – an 820 percent increase.

Naturally the explosion in population caused a burgeoning enrollment in the nation's schools. Enrollment of Consolidated No. 1 went from 200 to 500 within five years. Twenty years later (1969) the number reached 15,000.

Like other districts in the country, C-1 had a hard time keeping up with population growth. For several years, the five schools experienced overcrowding. Basements, gymnasiums, stages and hallways in the buildings were used as temporary classrooms. In 1950, voters approved a $72,000 bond issue for a music and industrial arts annex to Ruskin High School. Residents also approved free transportation for all district students.

In 1955 Union Point celebrated its 100th anniversary. More than 300 people attended the open house celebration, nine of whom went to Union Point before 1900. One of the nine was 91-year-old William H. Johnson (see page 40).

Shown here at Union Point's centennial celebration with six-year-old Cindy Freeman, a student at the school whose mother later served as president of the school board, Mr. Johnson attended Union Point in the 1860s and taught at the school at the turn of the century. While serving as Jackson County Superintendent of Schools, he helped convince Missouri lawmakers to pass the law that made school consolidation possible. Johnson Elementary School is named for Mr. Johnson.

Mid-century commitment to education was nationwide. The federal government, for example, subsidized school lunches, which brought the cost for each child to 20 cents per lunch. And in an effort to eliminate polio, considered the last major childhood pestilence, after vaccines largely eliminated diphtheria, measles and whooping cough, the government launched the largest vaccination program in history.

Polio attacked nerves in the brain and spinal cord. The first widespread blow to American children, killing 6,000 and paralyzing 27,000, was in 1916. Thereafter, every summer, parents lived in dread of the contagious disease. Later epidemics occurred in the 1940s and 1950s.

Westridge Elementary School, shown here, was near 104th Street on Grandview Road. Built for 360 students, grades 1- 6, the school's original plans called for 20 classrooms, but limited funds reduced that number to 12. Construction costs were $243,365, with an additional $26,276 for the land, grading, sewage disposal and equipment. (Total costs for Truman Elementary were $305,534.) When the school opened in the fall of 1956, 434 students were enrolled. By the time it was dedicated, two months later, another 16 students were added.

A Time To Celebrate

By the start of that important school year, 1953/54, the first 30 homes in a suburb called Ruskin Heights were occupied by families with 42 school-age children. Within six months, 1,000 additional new homes were built in the district. Crowded conditions, a post-war situation experienced by schools nationwide, forced the school board to reject admittance of non-resident students, who at one time paid tuition to attend the district schools. The following school year, as a space-saving measure, the board voted to eliminate kindergarten classes for the 1955/56 school year.

Despite three election campaigns, the school board could not convince voters to pass the necessary funding for a new elementary school. Many patrons questioned the huge expense of the proposed building. At a board meeting, Dr. George Englehart, the Missouri director of school building services, was invited to speak about the project's design and cost. One parent, eager to economize on the budget, asked him to describe a school building that would be more economical than the one proposed.

"I suppose," Dr. Englehart responded dryly, " a cell block would be more economical."

Opposition to the plan ended that night. In April 1953, voters approved a bond issue totaling $350,000 for a school, which would include 12 classrooms, a kindergarten room, all-purpose room, kitchen facilities, offices and a health room. Federal funds ($89,320) were used to add another wing with seven more classrooms. C.A. Burke School, the first modern

During the 1953/54 school year, Hickman Mills became one of the nation's trial districts for the first polio vaccines. With the assistance of PTA volunteers, children were bussed to clinics in Jackson County where health officials administered the vaccinations. The district's children were among 1.8 million selected in the trial. Dr. Jonas Salk, the vaccine's developer, became a national hero, when the test's successful results were announced the following year. Within a few years, polio in the U.S. was practically eliminated.

elementary school in the district, opened September 13, 1954, and was dedicated exactly 13 months later.

1955 was clearly a year to celebrate. Union Point, the district's oldest school and one of the original four to consolidate, held its 100th anniversary. The champion of consolidation, the district's native son, William H. Johnson, attended the widely publicized celebration.

More reasons for celebration came on January 22, 1955. A $600,000 bond issue passed overwhelmingly: 734 to 27. The special election was called to finance several new projects: an addition to the high school, and the construction of two new elementary schools.

When the school year began in the fall of 1955, more than 800 students walked into the consolidated district's third and largest – though not quite finished – high school building. The old high school – Ruskin #2 – became a junior high school for 7th and 8th graders. Built a few dozen yards east of the former school, the new Ruskin High School had 18

Construction on the 20-classroom Truman Elementary School (shown here), which was built for 600 students, began in June 1955. It opened on January 23, 1956, five days after construction ended. The next fall, when it was dedicated, 700 students, grades 2-6, were enrolled in the school.

That school year, the district distributed a teacher's manual that included a "Philosophy of Education," which, in part, stated,

"Each individual [pupil] must understand that with each privilege there comes a responsibility. [Underlining used in quoted source.] The American way of life recognizes as the three great contributing institutions the church, the home, and the school...

"Below will be found specific statements of desired attainments in the education experiences of the Ruskin School District:

(A) Development to the maximum of the child's mental, physical and social abilities.

(B) Lead to an awareness of the special interests and abilities, and develop them adequately for every child.

(C) Create a greater desire within the child to serve mankind unselfishly and efficiently.

(D) To produce a more physically fit generation through proper health training and clinical services provided through the schools.

(E) Development of the appreciation for the beauty of life and a deep respect for it.

(F) A keener desire to study and understand the problems of the world – political, economical, religious and social.

(G) Open the avenues for creative thinking; encourage initiative and develop ingenious ideas.

(H) Development of skills through vocational classes.

(I) An individual desirous of accepting the responsibilities of every good citizen, confident in his actions and unselfish in his endeavors.

(J) An awareness within the child that Christian principles must be applied if people are to live and work together in a compatible manner.

classrooms, a cafeteria, shop, music room and library. That same year the Fathers' Club erected bleachers at the high school's football field.

Construction in the district was non-stop. On January 23, 1956, Harry S. Truman Elementary School opened on James Reed Road, and on the western side of the district, Westridge Elementary School opened the following fall. Also in 1956, additions to the new high school were complete: four more classrooms, an auditorium and a gymnasium.

So much to celebrate

During American Education Week, on November 11, 1956, the community set aside a day to honor the good fortune of the 54-year-old district. That Sunday, the new Ruskin High School, and the Truman and Westridge Elementary Schools were dedicated. Former Pres. Harry S. Truman attended as the guest speaker. Students, faculty, and 800 parents and community leaders gathered in the new, state-of-the-art high school auditorium.

While introducing the guest speaker, Ruskin's principal, Marvin Langford, reminded the audience that Pres. Truman had "once farmed the land where Ruskin now stands."

It was a night to remember...for many reasons. Six months later, on the tragic night of May 20, 1957, all that remained of the November dedication site was just a wasteland – where two Ruskins once stood.

Photograph courtesy of Marjorie Langford

During its first year, the third Ruskin High School, built a short distance east of the former high school, had 19 teachers and 410 students. The next year, four additional classrooms and a gymnasium/auditorium were added to accommodate 550 students and 24 teachers. Construction and equipment for the school cost about $800,000, of which $210,000 were federal funds.

This photograph, showing Marvin Langford and former Pres. Harry S. Truman, was taken the day of the dedication ceremony on November 11, 1956, and is the only known photograph of the ill-fated high school building.

Chapter 6: The Tornado

Sometime in the late afternoon on May 20, 1957, a fierce storm hit Spring Hill, Kansas, a small town a little more than 10 miles south of Olathe. Someone spotted a funnel in the mass of black clouds, raw as a bruise and advancing toward the Missouri border.

As early as 6:00 p.m., radio and television announcers began alerting listeners. In an era before early-warning systems, the best hope of spreading the word was neighbor-calling-neighbor. The storm's speed – some estimates said 30 m.p.h., but in fact it was going much faster – made such primitive warnings tragically slow.

The funnel moved northeast, heading toward the center of Grandview, Missouri. But then it changed its path. Suddenly turning north, the whirling cloud clipped the northwest corner of Grandview, and then, spinning in a northeasterly course again, it followed the tracks of the Kansas City Southern Railroad, as if magnetized by the metal rails.

The twister was headed directly into Hickman Mills.

Some residents later remembered hearing an earth-trembling roar. Some heard the static popping of electric wires arcing together in pale blue explosions. Some heard a thousand freight trains.

At 7:35 p.m., it hit. With the fury of a runaway locomotive, the tornado roared into the heart of the village. Twelve minutes later it was over.

Photograph courtesy of the Jackson County Advocate

A tornado is a storm in which rotating winds are of severe intensity, and pressure is low and falls rapidly. This particular twister in 1957 was a multi-vortex funnel tornado, meaning that more than one vortex rotated around the main funnel. As true with all tornadoes in the northern hemisphere, the 1957 twister rotated counter-clockwise. It was an F5 tornado, the most intense on the Fujita Tornado Intensity scale. Fewer than five in 1,000 tornadoes are F5s. It traveled on the ground for 71 miles after picking up speed northeast of Williamsburg, Kansas, eventually reaching a speed of at least 50 m.p.h. (The average speed of a tornado is 30 m.p.h.) Continuing in a northeasterly direction, the funnel spun along the ground until it passed through Hickman Mills, Missouri, and then it rose and fell as it made its way further northeast. At Sibley, Missouri, the storm tore up barns, churches and homes, leaving $12,000 in damages before churning across the Missouri River and moving on.

Photograph courtesy of the Jackson County Advocate

The area most affected in Hickman Mills was between U.S. 71 and Raytown Road, and from Bannister Road and the intersection of Blue Ridge Extension and U.S. 71. Hardest hit of the destroyed homes were those between 109th and 112th streets in Ruskin Heights. The northwest part of Grandview and all of Martin City suffered damage.

Besides hundreds of destroyed homes in Hickman Mills, 16 businesses were completely leveled by the tornado. Most businesses south of 115th along the highway were seriously damaged. People who saw the tornado pound against large storefronts said that plate glass windows appeared to explode, as if a bomb inside had gone off.

The Praver & Sons Construction Company began rebuilding homes within a week of the tornado. Construction crews worked 12- to 14-hour days. Labor disputes, primarily over wages, hampered construction for several days during the early weeks.

Beginning in 1953 with nothing but farmland and using the post-war tract development in Levittown on Long Island, New York, as a model, Praver & Sons had developed Ruskin Heights suburb. The concept of fast-built, tract housing was new to Kansas City, but the enormous numbers of returning veterans after World War II and the Korean conflict were eager home buyers. By April 1956, Praver & Sons completed 1,840 single-family residences, using three to four architectural models, on 629 acres. Large crews could pour 25 slabs in one day. Basements were $1,500 extra. A three-bedroom, one-bath ranch with no basement cost about $10,000. Major appliances were included. Veterans did not need down payments.

The weather bureau said that the path of the tornado was a matter of chance. The odds of it happening again in Hickman Mills, the experts insisted, were about 10,000 to one. But many residents decided to err on the side of safety this time. Many who rebuilt in Ruskin Heights opted to put in a basement this time. Just in case.

Thirty-seven people were dead. Two died when their car was thrown aloft and smashed into the tank of the 100-foot water tower beside Burke Elementary School. Hundreds more were injured. More than 600 homes and two schools – Ruskin High School and Ruskin Junior High School – were completely destroyed and one, Burke, was seriously damaged. Fifty businesses, including all of Ruskin Shopping Center where 30 to 40 people were trapped under debris, were wiped out. Damage costs totaled more than $10 million.

Somewhere a little north of Bannister and Raytown Roads the tornado lifted, leaving a 10-mile swath of death and destruction. Trees not snapped off at ground level were stripped of leaves. Some upright trees were wrapped with twisted automobiles or other debris. The smell of gas was everywhere. Power lines lay across streets and yards. The danger was not over.

Volunteer efforts to help, which arrived that night, came from all over the country. In the days to come, people as far away as Iowa picked up utility bills, photographs, clothes and other personal objects owned by people from Hickman Mills and carried by the winds.

Today the only reminder of that tragic night is the memorial on 111th Street at the Blue Ridge Blvd. entrance to Ruskin Heights subdivision. The three arches in the brick wall of the memorial represent Faith, Hope and Love – the three elements that enabled the victims to survive the worst disaster in the community's history.

Photograph courtesy of the Jackson County Advocate

Missouri had known worse storms. On March 18, 1925, the deadliest tornado in American history tore through eastern Missouri, southern Illinois and southern Indiana, killing 689.

Approximately 12,000 people lived in the path of the 1957 tornado. According to The World Almanac and Book of Facts 2000, 48 people died in the storm. Significant Tornadoes, a book by Tom Grazulis, states that 531 were injured and 900 homes, businesses, churches and schools were destroyed or damaged. Six hundred of the homes were in Hickman Mills' Ruskin Heights subdivision. It was the most destructive disaster in western Missouri history.

The crumpled car shown here was thrown by the storm into the southwest side of the 100-foot water tower that stood near Burke Elementary School. (A shorter tower stands there today. After Kansas City annexed Hickman Mills in 1960, the tower was lowered for maximum use.) The child who died, and who was in the automobile, was found in the barbed wire separating the Kansas City Southern railroad tracks from Burke School.

Many houses in Ruskin Heights did not have basements. Dozens of people survived the storm because they took sanctuary in neighbors' basements. Sixty to 70 people lived through the storm in the Ruskin Heights Presbyterian Church. The church building, built a year and a half earlier, was totally demolished, but the main floor held, protecting the people beneath it.

Several people died after being hit by a freezer, a refrigerator, or other large appliance. Doctors later pulled roofing nails from the back of one woman survivor. Many years later when the woman lost feeling in her legs, surgeons at the Mayo Clinic found marble-size scar tissue against her spinal column. Doctors believed the tissue developed around paint chips and other storm debris that pierced the woman's body.

Photographs courtesy of the Jackson County Advocate

This well-known photograph, taken by Aggie Turnbaugh at the Jackson County Advocate newspaper, shows the eerie and ironic calling card left by the storm. The letters RU IN were among the few left on the gymnasium wall of Ruskin High School, built less than two years earlier. The two boys in the photograph were part of a contingency of student and teacher volunteers organized by Blaine Steck, the high school principal, two days after the storm. He asked them to scour the school grounds looking for salvageable school supplies and equipment. The recovered items were then taken to Truman Elementary School for storage.

The storm hit the day before graduation for 74 Ruskin High School seniors. Shortly after the storm, seven high schools in the metropolitan area called Steck to offer their auditoriums for Ruskin's delayed ceremony.

On May 24, Ruskin seniors received their diplomas in an emotional commencement held at Center High School in Kansas City, Missouri. The song, "Winds Across the Sky," originally scheduled, was cut from the program. A song that was performed, however, brought tears to the eyes of every person attending, according to Marjorie Langford, a teacher at Ruskin High School. The song was "You'll Never Walk Alone." The first line is "When you walk through a storm hold your head up high."

One graduate who received his diploma that night was James Kildow. His father, George, a custodian at Ruskin, had died in the storm, crushed by the collapsing walls at the school. Also killed was the school's nurse, Alta D. Guyll. Their bodies were found at 8:30 a.m. the morning after the storm. Although another custodian, Loren Ervin, and Blain Steck were also at Ruskin that night, they found sanctuary in the school's music room.

Ruskin High School, which was built in 1955 and is shown here in the aerial photograph, was completely destroyed. The old Ruskin, which was next door and was serving as a junior high school, was a wrecked shell. At the top left of the photograph barely damaged homes are visible, revealing the surgical precision of the storm's fury.

School officials estimated that damage to the three school buildings (Burke School was the third) was $2.7 million. This did not include the schools' contents. Plans for the next year's operations began the day after the storm. At first officials felt that junior and senior high school students should attend classes on a half-day basis in what remained of Burke. Two area churches offered their education classrooms to the school district. Within a few weeks, however, when reconstruction of Burke moved forward more rapidly than anticipated, new plans were announced for a full-day session in the fall for the upper grades at Burke.

Photograph courtesy of the Jackson County Advocate

Clean up of Burke Elementary School [shown here with the water tower in the background where two deaths occurred] began two days after the tornado. The storm destroyed one wing of the school, and ripped off one wall and a roof. Part of the school's auditorium collapsed and other areas were partially damaged. Playground equipment – climbing towers, swings and see-saws – was twisted freakishly.

Several boy scouts, meeting in the building that night, avoided injury when the troop leader corralled them into a hallway. Lloyd Kingcade, a custodian, had just left the wing when the funnel dropped on the school. He also sought safety in a corridor. About 200 feet south of the school, Kingcade later found the unclad body of a young woman.

When classes resumed in the fall, Burke students were evenly divided between Truman, Westridge and the recently built W.H. Johnson Elementary Schools. The schools' gymnasiums and stages were divided by partitions and served as 7th and 8th grade classrooms. The students from Ruskin High School attended classes at the rapidly restored Burke.

The photograph on the right shows remains of food lying in debris from a destroyed kitchen: coffee can with ground coffee, a pound of bacon in its wrapper, a loaf of wrapped bread, sealed jars of food.

"At some homes, not enough household articles," the Jackson County Advocate reported, "could be found to cover the top of a dining room table." At this home, leveled by the storm, a few household items remained miraculously intact.

By 2 a.m., the morning after the disaster, ambulances and emergency crews arrived in Hickman Mills, coming from a 50-mile-radius of the damaged area. At the height of the disaster, Menorah Hospital was forced to use hallways and the employees' dining room as additional emergency room space. Medical personnel reported that one of the most distressing sights that night was injured children brought to the hospital in the arms of strangers. The whereabouts of their parents, alive or dead, was unknown. Throughout the first night, surviving victims traveled from one emergency facility to the next trying to find missing relatives.

The next morning emergency organizations sent representatives to Hickman Mills. For example, more than 300 Red Cross workers, mostly volunteers, assisted with food, clothing, shelter and medical care. The Red Cross, which sent 23 officials from Washington D.C., launched a million-dollar campaign for tornado relief. Within a three-hour period on the day after the storm, the organization received $25,525.93.

Photograph courtesy of the Jackson County Advocate

Robert Shea, vice president of the American Red Cross, said, "I am impressed with the self-reliance of the people out there. And I have never seen a better example of a total community responding to the needs of part of the community. The tornado fund-drive progress is a tremendous example of community co-operation."

Of the more than 800 families in Missouri and Kansas applying for Red Cross aid, 475 were in the Ruskin Heights-Hickman Mills area.

Photograph courtesy of the Jackson County Advocate

Sympathetic response to victims was overwhelming. Scores of doctors and health care workers showed up at hospitals throughout the county to volunteer their services. Many physicians established first aid posts near the site. Nurses, doctors and wives of doctors opened a medical emergency treatment center at Richards-Gebaur Air Force Base. An entire dormitory of students at Rockhurst College showed up at Menorah Hospital, the city's southern-most medical facility and closest to Hickman Mills, to donate blood. Hearing about the shortage of ambulances, owners of station wagons lined up outside hospitals. They drove throughout the night, collecting the injured and dying.

Organizations of every kind started fundraising drives. Some included Westingtonhouse, IBM, Holsum Bread, Commerce Trust Company, Ford Motor Company, A & P Food Stores, Donnelly Garment Sales Company, Cook Paint and Varnish, the UAW, AFL-CIO, International Brotherhood of Boilermakers, and Armco Foundation.

About 50 Mennonites came from Kansas to help with the clean up. They did whatever a resident needed, no job was too large or too small – from raking trash to hauling away boulder-size rubble. When one homeowner, who had nothing left but a concrete foundation, asked what he could pay the Mennonite helping him, the volunteer just asked for a photograph of the new house after it was built.

Churches, schools and private homes opened to admit homeless victims. Priests and preachers toured the ruins. During the chaotic first night, one priest reported performing a baptism using water from the radiator of a storm-twisted car.

Archives of the Jackson County, Missouri Historical Society

This was one of four canteens operating in the storm area. Three mobile canteens, providing sandwiches and other food and comfort items, were opened within two days of the storm.

The day after the storm, long distance operators reported handling 67,551 outgoing calls. It was a record for a 24-hour period. Normally operators received 34,000 calls daily. Local calls also rose. Southwestern Bell Telephone Company said that on May 21st telephone use jumped 35 to 85 percent.

Southwestern Bell replaced 28,000 feet of aerial feeder cable and 325 poles knocked down during the storm. By May 23, the company restored phones to the 7,000 customers who lost service.

Within 48 hours of the storm, gas and electric services in the stricken area were back. Two hundred workers – that is, all Kansas City Power and Light's available crews – replaced 120 poles in that two day period. The company estimated that the storm knocked down about 27 miles of wiring.

Gas Service Company workers toured the devastated area, looking for possible trouble spots. The gas company estimated that 500 to 600 of the homes that it had once served had vanished in the storm. Miraculously the storm's destruction created no gas fires or injuries due to leaking gas.

Taking their cue from a popular song by Elvis Presley, the owners of this damaged house wrote on the door, "I'm All Shook Up. Smiths." Storm victims needed such a sense of humor to face some of the indignities and outrages in the days ahead:

Photograph courtesy of the Jackson County Advocate

Looters descended on the devastated area during the first night. A government official, inspecting the storm scene about 30 minutes after the funnel left, reported seeing looters in the shopping center, taking goods from the drug store, supermarket and other shops. One person was carrying out a cash register. Some looters brought trucks to haul away large, still-intact appliances strewn over residential areas. Seven men were arrested for looting during the second night. When reconstruction began, looters also stole lumber and building supplies.

One resident, whose home blew away, remembers finding only a handful of his possessions after the storm, including a beaten up washbasin found in a neighbor's yard. The man put the basin on the slab of his former house, intending to save it as a memento. That night looters stole it.

Law enforcement officials estimated 250,000 sightseers passed through the area on a single day shortly after the storm. The traffic greatly hindered salvage and rebuilding efforts. Some residents of Ruskin Heights remembered seeing commercial airplanes circling overhead, as if the disaster site had become a national tourist attraction.

To prevent looting and reduce traffic jams caused by sightseers, Missouri Gov. James Blair declared martial law at 10:10 p.m. the night of the storm. All available sheriff's deputies, civil defense workers, National Guard, 50 police officers, 100 to 150 state troopers and 200 airmen from Richards-Gebaur Air Force Base helped maintain the 7 p.m. curfew and kept looters and sightseers at bay. Storm victims registered at the Grandview Community Hall to receive identification cards, allowing them access to and from the restricted disaster area.

Photograph courtesy of the Jackson County Advocate

Despite severe damage to their car, one couple [shown here] managed to smile in the midst of the devastation. There were many things – curiosities of an unpredictable twister – that revealed elements of macabre comedy in an otherwise wholly tragic event...

- *In one home, destroyed by the storm, rescuers found a bedside table still standing with a goldfish bowl on top. The fish inside was alive.*
- *In another freakish occurrence, a pan from a bakery in the shopping center smashed through the exterior shingles and wall of a home, barely missing a woman hiding under an iron bed. The woman survived, although she was nearly sucked from beneath the bed when the low-pressure center of the funnel passed overhead.*
- *The A & P Food Store was located in Ruskin Shopping Center, a two-million dollar complex built only two and a half years earlier. The storm tore off the store's roof and walls. In one of the many bizarre incidents from the storm, cans and bottles of food, some still in sacks, stood on the check-out counter, where fleeing customers left them when the storm hit.*
- *Cleaning up after a storm that had the power to rip the asphalt tile off a kitchen floor, one volunteer at the high school found an unbroken light bulb lying in the parking lot.*
- *On May 21, farmers near Chillicothe, Missouri, picked up debris from the Hickman Mills storm. Photographs, canceled checks, bits of wallpaper and insulation, atlases, family Bibles, telephone directories and other identifiable items, were swept for miles in the vortex of the raging twister. Twenty-five miles north of Chillicothe people found songbooks from a Ruskin Heights church. Letters and receipts from Hickman Mills were found in Richmond, Missouri.*

The handwritten sign on the door shown here advertises, "Devines lived here. Slightly used lumber & furniture (cheap.)" Nearby is another sign beside a mannequin covered in a sheet to resemble a corpse. The sign's message: "Here Lies Our Mortgage."

Two days after the storm, Missouri Gov. James Blair met in Kansas City, Missouri, with Mayor H. Roe Bartle, the city manager, the police chief, the police board president, and officials of the federal Civil Defense Agency. After the meeting, Gov. Blair sent a letter to Pres. Dwight Eisenhower:

> Disastrous tornado struck southern edge of Metropolitan Kansas City last night inflicting heavy damage and causing great loss of life. Damage, hardship and suffering so severe that federal assistance is required to supplement the efforts of state and local authorities including Civil Defense organizations.
>
> Red Cross and other charitable institutions are rendering full assistance. Respectfully suggest allocations of 25 million dollars of funds available to you under authority of Public Law 875, 81st Congress. Your favorable consideration of this request will be deeply and gratefully appreciated by the unfortunate residents of this disaster stricken area.

The amount requested was the same figure provided by the Truman administration after the local flood in 1951.

More than 1,000 residents, some wearing bandages from injuries suffered in the storm, attended a mass meeting at Ruskin Heights Shopping Center on May 25, 1957, to learn about receiving disaster and rehabilitation aid from officials of the Red Cross, Salvation Army, the National Guard, federal agencies, various banking and loan associations, several churches and law enforcement.

Photograph courtesy of the Jackson County Advocate

Photograph courtesy of the Jackson County Advocate

On May 18, 1958, a year after the tornado, the community held a commemorative service. U.S. Sen. Stuart Symington, for whom one of the district's elementary schools is named, was the guest speaker. Shown here greeting local boy scouts, Sen. Symington had acted as liaison between the storm-stricken area and the Eisenhower administration in order to secure federal funds for storm relief. About 2,000 people attended the May, 1958, event at which the brick memorial was dedicated to those killed in the storm.

A few months later, on November 19, a "Tornado Dinner" was given at the newly rebuilt Ruskin High School gymnasium. The dinner honored the organizations and individuals who helped after the storm. Sponsors of the event included the Hickman Mills Chamber of Commerce, the Optimist Club, American Legion Post #598 and the school board of Consolidated #1. Prior to dinner, a motor tour was made of the disaster area. Dignitaries invited to the dinner included Mayor H. Roe Bartle, Sen. Stuart Symington and Harry and Bess Truman.

With the rubble cleared away, a new Ruskin High School was built in a little more than 10 months after the tornado. A similar project normally required two or two and a half years. Federal disaster aid provided $1,100,093 and insurance another $850,000 toward its construction.

Built of reinforced concrete, the new school had a distinctive feature: its middle floor was built first, before the ground floor or the proposed third floor. This was in response to federal regulations, which stipulated that the district could not use federal funds to rebuild a structure larger than the one that the district had lost in the tornado. Consequently, the building's designers put in an 11-foot-tall "crawl space," which eventually became the school's first floor. The structure also allowed for a third floor addition in order to accommodate a projected enrollment of 3,000.

Also unusual, even ironical, was the fact that the district still continued to pay off the debt on the destroyed building, although there was no debt on the new building. The new Ruskin High School was free and clear.

CHAPTER 7: EXPANSION

Photograh: Dance (late 1950s) at concession stand #2 in Kernodle Park, a popular social destination for Hickman Mills teenagers.

Photograph courtesy of the Kernodle family

On January 1, 1961, the U. S. Post Office no longer recognized the Hickman Mills name. The village officially ceased to exist. Kansas City, Missouri, had annexed the little village.

Throughout the previous year, campaigns to prevent annexation were intense and often divisive. The village did not have the kinds of services that communities in mid-20th century America had come to expect. It lacked its own police force, municipal officers, sewage disposal program and fire department (other than a volunteer one). Most voters wanted these amenities. They approved annexation. And so at the start of the new year, Kansas City, that great leviathan to the north, which had all those modern services and more, swallowed up everything.

Everything, that is, but the school system. From that time forward, the Hickman Mills C-1 School District became the unifying force of the community.

It *was* the community.

Certainly the tornado, three years earlier, helped solidify a deep sense of community spirit. Marjorie Langford, whose home was within two blocks of Burke School, had huddled in the basement with her young son during the tornado and was knocked unconscious by a freezer. A teacher at Ruskin High School, Langford remembered, "The next few years after the tornado were remarkable. They were some of the best years of my time with the school district. Everyone pulled together – students, faculty, administration, parents. We were a close knit, caring community."

Photograph appeared in the Kansas City Star, February 18, 1950.

In 1950, Jerry Atwood, a student at Ruskin High School, came to class with a Mohawk haircut, a narrow strip of hair running from his forehead to his neck in the back. As a front-page article in The Kansas City Star *explained, "School officials told him he could not go to classes until the hair was cut in a presentable fashion." In protest of Atwood's expulsion, fellow students walked out of classes for three hours.*

Officials allowed Atwood to return to school after he trimmed the Mohawk from one-inch tall to 1/2 inch. Other students in The Kansas City Star *photograph are (left to right) Howard Benjamin, Tommy Hudgens (standing) and Helen Benjamin. "The haircut was the result of a dare by Howard Benjamin and Hudgens," said the newspaper article.*

The Benjamin family were among the earliest settlers in the Hickman Mills area. Hyman Benjamin came to Missouri in the mid 1800s. He bought 40 acres at three dollars an acre, which grew to more than 200 acres by 1890. His was one of the county's most prosperous dairy farms, known as Benjamin Ranch. Still operating today, the ranch operates a 3,000 seat outdoor theater, a 6,000 seat rodeo arena and four barns open for commercial use. The ranch hosts more than 600 events annually and attracts more than 150,000 visitors.

As the community's primary focal point, Hickman Mills was one of the fastest growing school districts in Missouri. Its enrollment skyrocketed 783 percent from 1950 to 1958. Ruskin High School had 100 seniors in 1958, with more than 850 first graders enrolling in the same year. At that time, there were 5,000 homes in the district and another 5,000 planned for the near future. In the constellation of neighborhoods that increasingly fell within the province of Kansas City, Missouri, Hickman Mills was one of its brightest stars.

The Ruskin Golden Eagle Band's trip to the Rose Bowl in Pasadena, California, lasted from December 26 to January 3, 1960, and involved 81 band members [shown here marching in the Rose Bowl] and about 10 chaperons. The cost, $14,970, included $8,760 in railroad tickets, hotel, 20 uniform replacements, a banner, a new bass horn and a tour of Marineland. The money was raised through various fundraisers, including a Rodeo Kids Show, Ozark Jubilee Show, Truman Corners Day, Folgers Coffee Day and a Lions Club Benefit. Sponsors of the trip were the local Chamber of Commerce, the Ruskin Flower and Garden Club, Optimist Club, Junior Chamber of Commerce, Ruskin Shopping Center, American Legion Memorial Post 598, Truman Corners Shopping Center, Milgram Food Stores, the C-1 school board, Ruskin Heights Presbyterian church, Ruskin Heights Baptist Church, Ruskin Heights Lutheran Church, Longview Methodist Church and Hickman Mills Community Christian Church.

On January 1, television network, NBC, selected Ruskin's Golden Eagle Band for a special pre-parade nationwide feature. Later, during the Rose Bowl game, Blaine Steck, Ruskin's principal who traveled with the band, caught one of the game footballs kicked into the crowd after a touchdown. Band members autographed the football, which was placed in the school's trophy case as a memento of the trip. Later that spring, the president of the Pasadena Tournament of Roses Association visited Ruskin and presented the band with a trophy for being chosen the outstanding high school band at the parade.

In 1975, the Ruskin Golden Eagles performed at the Orange Bowl in Miami, Florida. Three years later, the well-traveled band marched again in the Rose Bowl.

Growing ~ Troubles and Triumphs

Such extraordinary growth was bound to create tensions.

In 1957 and 1958, the six-person school board split into two equal factions, causing stalemates on several important issues, notably on hiring/firing policies and on lines of authority. The controversies led to the resignations of three superintendents within a seven-year period. In late 1958, more than 2,500 worried residents signed petitions asking that all board members resign. Again the board divided three to three on accepting the citizens' request.

Finally on February 19, 1959, the board adopted a resolution inviting the National Commission for the Defense of Democracy Through Education from the National Education Association "to make an investigation of the relationship that previously existed between this Board and the Boards of Education in both administrations and the superintendent; and between the superintendents and the employed personnel of the school district during the past two administrations."

The Washington D.C.-based NEA commission agreed to investigate. Following three days (May 15-18, 1960) of interviews, the commission reviewed questionnaires sent to 320 district employees and patrons. Made up of seven education professionals from across the U.S. and a four-person staff, the commission issued its findings on February 1, 1960, at a public meeting in Ruskin High School. The *Jackson County Advocate*, one of several news organizations covering the standing-room-only event, called it "a tense and dramatic report session."

The detailed 37-page report focused on three main areas: an analysis of the problem, findings, and suggestions. Each area outlined specific criticisms and suggestions for everyone connected with the consolidated district – Board of Education, Superintendent of Schools, Administrative Council (a group made up of the superintendent, school principals, the curriculum director, purchasing agent and president of the Community Teachers Association), teachers and district residents. The outcome of the commission's recommendation led to the resignation of the school board president; the adoption of a district handbook detailing administrative rules and regulations; the strengthening of the superintendent's responsibilities and functions; and the termination of all standing committees, with the proviso that future committees be appointed for specific and temporary tasks.

In the midst of solving growing pains, the district struggled with providing sufficient classroom space for its ever-expanding enrollment. From the summer after the tornado through the 1960s, Hickman Mills C-1 School District not only rebuilt two schools and restored another, it also constructed eight new schools: Johnson Elementary (1957), Symington Elementary (1959), Baptiste Junior High (1959), Warford Elementary (1961), Dobbs Elementary (1962), Ervin Junior High (1963), Ingels Elementary (1966), and Smith-Hale Junior High (1968).

Even in the midst of administration problems, the district's residents continued their commitment to the growing school system and its children. In 1960, less than six weeks after the PTA endorsed the school board's letter inviting the NEA to investigate, a general election was held regarding reassessment of property taxes. On April 7, a heavy voter turn out resulted in the approval of the highest tax assessment for schools in the history of Jackson County.

ACHIEVEMENTS DID NOT END WITH BRICKS AND MORTAR

In June 1960, the Hickman Mills C-1 School District received Missouri's highest rating, AAA. (Formerly the district had an AA rating.)

Around this time, WDAF-TV broadcast a scholastic-based game show for area students. Ruskin High School often sent a team to the competition.

"We won repeatedly," Marjorie Langford remembered. "Show after show."

Two elementary schools outside the district (South City View School, which no longer exists, was near today's Mt. Moriah cemetery, and Boone School which is still at Wornall and 89th Street) were small, independent education systems. Because those districts had no high schools, their grade school graduates had the option of attending either the Center School District or Hickman Mills C-1 School District. Each student's old district paid a tuition fee. The majority chose to attend Hickman Mills, which eventually stopped accepting students outside its boundaries due to increased enrollment within its own population.

Photograph courtesy of the Kernodle family

A 1949 article in the Hi-Light, Ruskin High School's newspaper, advised girls about fashion: "Girls, now is the time to dress like a princess because taffetas, satin, and velvet are in style. The fashion colors are emerald green, midnight blue, and steel gray. You can get `hug me tights' and beret hat to decorate. Attractive jewelry worn by Ruskin gals include charm bracelets, scatter pins and chokers."

Dressing like a princess and winning beauty contests were highly regarded goals for many women during the mid 20th century. The photograph here was used to promote an annual beauty contest held at Kernodle Park. A popular recreational area for several decades, the park was located near today's Warford Elementary School.

In an advertisement in The Kansas City Star, *the 225-acre Kernodle Park, which was opened only for white people, was described as "Three lakes, 60 acres of water, 25-acre lake for use of motor boats and water skiing. Lakes are stocked with Bass, Crappie, Blue Gill, Minn. Catfish and Channel Cat.* *[Newspaper quotation continues on next page.]*

"Swimming area can accommodate over 1,000 people at same time. Bath house, concession stands, sandwiches, soft drinks, popcorn, sun-lounge chairs. Sand beach and grass beach. Kiddies pool. Water slides, surfboards, canoes. Juke box for dancing in bathing suit, Water basketball. Nursery where you can park the kiddies…

"Numerous picnic areas around lakes, beautiful spots with ovens and tables. One area has swings and kiddies merry-go-round. Two spots for soft ball and large group picnics (tables 50 feet long). Shelter house 30x80 feet with large fireplace. (Ideal for large group picnics in case of rain.)

"The original 70 acres of land was homesteaded by our maternal grandfather (Wiley Jones) in 1846 and the original govt. land patent direct from the Louisiana Purchase has been in our family ever since. Wiley Jones built the first school on the exact spot where our swimming pool now is located and it was known as `Coon Holler" school. Later this was moved to Hickman school."

Photograph courtesy of the Kernodle family

On July 27, 1966, Kernodle Park's racial segregation policy was challenged when a black Marine sergeant showed up at the park entrance and was turned away. Sgt. Frederick Peoples filed a complaint under the Missouri Public Accommodations law. In a long discrimination battle, the Kernodle family fought to keep the recreational facility segregated. When legal efforts failed, Jim Kernodle, the owner and shown driving the car on the opposite page, turned the property's operation over to the Kansas City Citizens Council, an all-white group to which Kernodle belonged. The park was finally opened to blacks in 1973.

During the heat of the NEA controversy, Ruskin High School received one of the highest honors in its history. The school's band was invited to perform at the Pasadena Tournament of Roses Parade on January 1, 1960. The Golden Eagle band was the first in Missouri to receive such an invitation and was the only high school outside the state of California participating in the event. Planning and funding for the California trip came from faculty, parents and businesses throughout the district.

Only one unsettling incident occurred on the trip. One of the students became ill on the train and underwent an appendectomy in a La Junta, Colorado, hospital. A school nurse traveling with the band, Hazel Dobbs (Dobbs Elementary School is named for her) stayed at the hospital until the student's parents arrived.

The entire object of true education is to make people not merely do the right things but to enjoy the right things.

– John Ruskin

On September 2, 1957, Arkansas Gov. Orval Faubus called in the National Guard to prevent black students from entering Little Rock's Central High School. His actions and the ensuing racial violence forced Pres. Dwight Eisenhower to send federal marshals to escort the black students into Central and to maintain a guard at the school.

The next year on September 29, the Supreme Court ruled that states could not create "evasive schemes" to maintain racial segregation. This dealt a deathblow to racially motivated plans in Arkansas and other states that involved leasing public schools to private organizations.

And so began one of the 20th century's most searing social struggles.

Located at 10900 Marsh, William H. Johnson Elementary School [shown here] opened on September 3, 1957. It was named for William Johnson, who attended Union Point in the 1800s and was a leading proponent of Missouri's 1901 school consolidation law. Mr. Johnson, who attended the 1957 dedication, died four years later at the age of 97.

One wall of the building, which was under construction during the 1957 tornado, was knocked down by the storm. The district's 1958 Annual Report featured two sections called "Storm Losses" and "Storm Gains." The first item under the latter section was "Burke reconstruction and minor repair to construction of Johnson done in 3 months' time. No cost – completely covered by insurance."

Long ignored, the lines separating black from white students throughout the country were suddenly center stage. Although the south received the spotlight, the midwest was also a hotbed of racial tensions. In 1923, Oklahoma was put under martial law by Gov. John Walton after terrorist activities of the Ku Klux Klan. The Klan had become a political force in the region. Several newspapers began exposing the group, its violence and subversive activities.

Certainly the divisions between the races in Jackson County, Missouri, had simmered since the border bloodbaths of the Civil War.

"The only [controversial] issue that I know of and the one that bothered me was the Ku Klux Klan in the early 1920s," Stephen Slaughter wrote in his family's history. "One Sunday night during the [Hickman Mills] church service, an American flag was brought into the church by several white-robed men and presented to the minister, King Stark. He made a few complimentary remarks and the men left. Soon after, several men, the same ones no doubt, came into the church with no robes and sat down and listened to the sermon.

"I was strong against the Klan and at home during vacation one summer I made scathing remarks about the Klan in Sunday school when classes were over and all were listening. My father [O.V., one of C-1's founders] was never a member, but one night after he had gone to bed a number of them called and practically drug him out of bed... However, I believe little was said in the community after I had made my impromptu talk in Sunday school, certainly no more men in white robes ever came to the church."

Slaughter's description of the incident in the church is indicative of the times. The 1920s and early 30s are often remembered as an era of rising crime rates and gangster operations, with Kansas City notorious for its mob activity. The depression and drought of the 1930s only exacerbated the social problems. Add racial tensions to the mix, and this era represented one of the most horrific in the nation's history. In fact, racial tensions in the midwest during the 1920s and into the 1930s reached epic proportions.

Schools were among one of the first public institutions to feel those tensions.

A 1959 Handbook for Teachers, published by the district's Administrative Office, listed these job duties:

1. *Carry on an adequate instructional program geared to the children in the room.*
2. *Give corporal punishment with adult witness, preferably the principal. File written report to the Central Office through the principal.*
3. *Stand at doorway to room during "passing period," and before and after school.*
4. *Any teacher may reprimand any child in school.*
5. *Keep case studies.*
6. *Report all strangers in building to principal.*
7. *Investigate to see if any child cannot take corporal punishment.*
8. *Never excuse a child from school without consulting the principal.*
9. *If and when a child is sent to the principal, send a written report of the specific reason or reasons.*
10. *Never strike a child about the head or pull his hair. Use the place nature provided. Group punishment for actions of a few will not be supported.*

Stuart Symington Elementary School [shown here] at 8650 Ruskin Way was completed in January 1959. Located in the heart of the tornado-ravaged Ruskin Heights subdivision, the school's name honored Missouri's U.S. Sen. Stuart Symington who helped facilitate access to emergency relief after the 1957 storm.

Educational apartheid was the law of the land. A little known court case made it the law. In 1899, the school district in Augusta, Georgia, closed its schools that were formerly available for black students, claiming that the district could no longer afford to keep them open. White schools remained operating. Black residents battled against the decision – all the way to the Supreme Court.

Three years earlier the court had decreed in *Plessy v. Ferguson* that public accommodations must be "separate but equal." The Augusta case, *Cumming v. Richmond County Board of Education*, now turned that issue to determine whether blacks had the constitutional right to receive from a public school system, an equal, albeit separate, public education. The court ruled no. Augusta had the right to shut down its schools for blacks, while leaving its schools for whites open.

Ben Ervin, whose family served on the Hickman Mills school board for several generations in the first half of the 20th century, remembered an early racial incident in the district.

"Sometime in the 1930s," Ervin said, "a black family moved into the Hickman Mills School District. The family, which included school-aged children, came from Kansas City. They were brought in as farm laborers by a man named Chester Washer, who owned an orchard across the road from Hickman School. Shortly after the black family's arrival, the district's board of education sent representatives to tell Washer that the family couldn't stay in the district. There were no schools for the children, he was told. The black family returned to Kansas City soon afterward."

Hickman Mills C-1 School District was under no obligation to create a school for the black workers' children. But a change was coming. In the early 1930s, the National Association for the Advancement of Colored People initiated a series of legal challenges to laws fostering "unequal" education. The NAACP particularly targeted graduate schools that denied blacks entry and public schools that paid black teachers a lower wage than white teachers. In 1938, the organization won a case against Missouri. The U.S. Supreme Court ruled that the state's failure to provide a law school for blacks was unconstitutional. It was a small victory with big consequences.

The pressure that this case, and many like it, created within the nation's educational communities paved the way for the seminal anti-discrimination case regarding school desegregation.

But it took 58 years. Finally on May 17, 1954, the Supreme Court struck down the "separate but equal" doctrine. The high court unanimously ruled that segregating children by race in public schools violated black children's constitutional right to equal protection under the law. Twenty-one states, Missouri included, fought the ruling of *Brown v. Board of Education of Topeka.*

Rulings of the court were slow to create practical changes within society. During the 1950s, metropolitan Jackson County remained entirely segregated residentially. Even the Kansas City Fire Department, until 1958, operated five, all-black companies. Until 1964, the popular Fairyland Amusement Park at 75th and Prospect Ave. only admitted black people to the park one day a year.

"People who were not here a generation ago scarcely can imagine how deeply racial segregation was embedded in the fabric of Kansas City," *The Kansas City Star* later reported in 1991. "The schools were entirely separate. Blacks were not served in restaurants and were turned away at hotels....

"Blacks simply weren't seen on the Plaza or, indeed, were hardly seen south of 31st Street unless they were in a maid's uniform or pushing a broom."

On April 23, 1964, Kansas City, Missouri, voters passed a Public Accommodations ordinance that desegregated hotels and restaurants. The measure barely squeaked by. Of the 90,000 votes cast, only a slim 2,614 votes made the difference. The next year, the Missouri legislature passed a statewide version of the measure.

On July 12, the year of the tornado, the Hickman Mills C-1 School District accepted a grant of land from Dr. Mary Baptiste, who had lived on the farm for 34 years. According to the agreement, the donated land – 15 acres of the northwest portion of the Baptiste estate – was to be used for non-profit purposes and for human welfare purposes.

In September 1959, Baptiste Junior High School (5401 East 103rd Street) opened. Classroom space for the district was so scarce that classes at the new school started while construction was still in progress. Like Ruskin High School, Baptiste was built to accommodate a third floor and a projected 3,000-pupil capacity.

The area around the junior high school was still rural. Roscoe Bernard, the school's first principal, remembered that one warm fall day, when the double doors in the back of the school were opened to let in a breeze, a horse wandered into the building, down the hallway and into two busy classrooms. The horse's name was Bud and belonged to Dr. Mary Baptiste, who still lived in a house nearby.

Baptiste was closed in 1982 and leased to a nearby company, Marion Laboratory. The district reopened the building for education purposes in 1998. Baptiste Educational Center eventually became the home of several programs, including the Management II School, PEP/CODE/ACE, Baptiste Day School and the Freda Markley Early Childhood Center.

GROWTH CONTINUED

Dr. Mary Baptiste was a biologist who patented liquid soap. Until 1954, she was the president of United Chemical of Kansas City, Missouri. She and her husband founded the company in 1913. For many years the Baptistes opened their Hickman Mills property, called Sleepy Hollow, for public use for philanthropic organizations such as the Red Cross and the Girl Scouts. The couple promised each other that, at their deaths, the farm would continue to be used for public good.

"I don't intend for the land ever to be commercialized," she said, after her husband's death in 1944. "I won't go back on my promise."

In 1941 the couple offered to give the 55-acre property, at that time valued at $100,000, to any organization that promised to maintain it and to assure that it be used for "physical, moral and spiritual betterment." No group qualified — the maintenance costs were too high ($5,000 to $10,000 annually.)

In 1957, Dr. Baptiste gave the school 15 acres of her farm. "I hesitated about the school because I didn't want to divide up the place," she said, "but I feel the outdoors is an important cultural and educational part of every child's growing up."

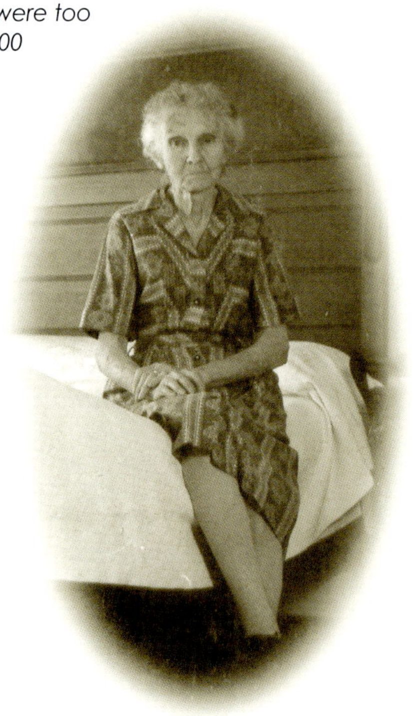

Despite the eight new schools constructed by the Hickman Mills C-1 School District between 1957 and 1968, enrollment kept one jump ahead of building projects. In the 1964/65 school year, most classrooms were packed beyond capacity with 40 or more students. Seniors graduating from Ruskin that year totaled 457. Confident that the district could handle its own fast-paced growth, voters in 1964 overwhelmingly rejected a proposal to merge with the Kansas City, Missouri School District. The issue brought the largest voter turn out in the district's history.

But enrollment numbers did not let up. The next school year, 1965/66, total enrollment was 11,846. Two years later, it reached 13,789. The 1967/68 statistics bore out what everyone knew was happening: the growth rate at C-1 was almost 1,000 students per year.

The following school year began as other recent years had begun: rising enrollment and overcrowding. Also like other years in the 1960s, it was a year rife with Vietnam War protests, political assassinations, and continuing racial tensions.

But there was one remarkable change. The district's 1968/69 school year began with two new enrollees: Robert Jr. and Gay-linn Gatewood. They were the first black students to enter Hickman Mills C-1 School District. Eighth grader Robert Jr. enrolled at Baptiste Junior High School, and Gay-linn at Westridge Elementary School.

In 1968, Robert and Ida Gatewood and their two children became the first black family to own a home in the district.

Mr. Gatewood remembered that his immediate neighbors made a point of making him and his family feel welcome. But there was also trouble.

"While we were moving in," he recalled, "a white man came to the door and said this was a mistake – our owning the house. He said he himself had made an offer to the former owners. At that time, the policy on buying a house was first-come-first-served. I had already made the down payment and been approved. I knew the man represented a contingent of people who hoped to stop our taking possession of the property, but I was the first with the payment and the policy prevailed. I was, however, the last to benefit from that policy. From that day on it changed. The new policy stipulated that by a given date several people could make an offer, put down a deposit and get approved. Then all their names would be put into a hat and the 'winner' selected. As my real estate agent said, we'd never have got the house in a lottery like that."

Shortly after the Gatewoods enrolled in the district, Carolyn Brock became the first black student at Ruskin High School. Because she was the only black person at the school, her parents did an extraordinary thing to help her succeed in the all-white environment. The Brock family brought Carolyn's cousin to live with them and to attend school with Carolyn. The overcrowded district, however, had very strict residency rules. Many families had moved to Hickman Mills expressly so that their children could attend the highly respected, as well as filled-beyond-capacity, schools. District rules specified, however, that only the children of residents could enroll in C-1. Consequently, the Brocks legally adopted the cousin so that she could attend Ruskin with Carolyn.

Despite its historic significance, *Brown v. the Board of Education* failed to provide sufficient guidelines for school desegregation. In pursuant rulings, the Supreme Court set forth milestones for achieving racial balance within districts. In the 1971 *Swann v. Charlotte-Mecklenburg Board of Education* case, the court ruled in favor of mandatory busing, rezoning of attendance boundaries and restricted use of quotas in order to achieve racial parity within individual schools. In short, communities were obliged to attain district-wide racial mixing and to attain it school by school. Busing was the centerpiece of the stratagem.

In the early 20th century, nine out of 10 black people lived in the south. Although a shift in demographics occurred following World War I, the real turning point came at the outbreak of World War II. There was a dramatic migration of southern black people to job markets in northern and western cities, especially to places like Kansas City with major war plants.

Statistics released by the U.S. Census in 1970 provided a snapshot of the average Hickman Mills resident during the previous 10 years. The average family income in the district was $12,359. (The median personal income of Jackson County in 1969 was $10,128.) The average education level of Hickman Mills residents was 12.49. Unemployment was lower than the national average of 2.19 percent. The community's age range was 45.9 percent between 15-44 years old and 27.4 percent between 5-14. None were black, until the Robert Gatewood family moved into the district in 1968.

That was the worst year for racial tensions in Kansas City's history. Widespread and violent protests ignited when city officials would not close Kansas City Public Schools in deference to the murder of Martin Luther King Jr., who was shot in April of that year. About 300 black students marched on city hall. That evening the entire 900-person police force, 168 state troopers and 1,700 National Guard were called in to quell riots in the streets. Within two days, seven people were dead, 54 injured and 175 arrested. National Guard was then increased to 2,200. Gov. Warren Hearnes sent in an additional 700 troopers. Before it ended two days later, more than 200 businesses were damaged, 75 fires started, and 275 people arrested.

The photograph shown here of Robert Gatewood Jr. [lower left] appeared in the Leprechaun, Baptiste Junior High School's yearbook, 1968. Gay-linn, his sister, was a third grader at Westridge Elementary School. The two were the first African American students in the C-1 school district.

During her senior year in 1976, Gay-linn became the first black student in the district to serve as editor of a school's yearbook. Gay-linn, who was graduated in 1976, remembered, "There were about 500 seniors that year. I was one of about 10 black students."

The Urban League of Greater Kansas City, in its 1991 report, The State of Black Kansas City, *estimated that by 2010 30 percent of people in Missouri between the ages of 18 and 24 will be non-Euro-ethnic.*

Elsie M. Warford Elementary School was built near Kernodle Park, the location of the Jones School, which along with Hedges School, combined to create Hickman School, one of the original four grade schools in the district. Located at 11400 Cleveland (formerly Annie Pate Road), the school was dedicated on December 3, 1961. It was named for Rockford School's best-known teacher, Elsie Warford, who retired in 1959 after more than 25 years at the school.

Hazel F. Dobbs Elementary School is located at 9400 Eastern. Like many schools built during this period, Dobbs was still under construction when students first arrived in the new building. According to the school's dedication program, "Construction was started in March, 1962, and completed sufficiently for occupation in early October, 1962." The school was named in memory of Hazel Dobbs, a former school nurse in the district. She founded the district's health and nursing service. After her death, a scholarship fund honoring her was administered by Ruskin High School.

THE RULING MET A WAVE OF CHALLENGES

A 1975 study by the Missouri Human Rights Commission pinpointed the desegregation challenge faced by districts like Hickman Mills. The study, called "Integration in Missouri Public Schools: Faculty and Students Twenty Years After Brown," revealed that 63 percent of the schools in greater Kansas City, Missouri, had student bodies with 95 percent or more of one race.

Since that time, minority families have continued to move to the Hickman Mills area, and the enrollment of their children in all the district's schools has increased through the years. The trend was countywide. By the 1990s, the number of black children attending formerly segregated schools in Jackson County had increased dramatically. In 1991, with blacks making up 37 percent of its enrollment, Hickman Mills had the third largest black student population in the metropolitan area. Only Kansas City, Missouri, and Kansas City, Kansas, had higher percentages.

Ervin Junior High School [shown here] opened in the fall of 1963. Located at 10530 Greenwood Road, the school was named for one of the earliest pioneer families in the district. Benjamin Franklin (Frank) Ervin served as the district's first board president. His daughter was in the first graduating class of Ruskin High School. During the first half of the 20th century, Frank Ervin's son and grandson were also members of the school board. The year after Ervin Junior High School opened an additional wing was added to the building.

Harry W. Ingels Elementary School, at 11600 Food Lane, was built in a record eight months. The school was named for Harry Ingels, the principal of Johnson Elementary School from September 1, 1957 to January 29, 1963. Mr. Ingels, who was 45 years old, died suddenly while at work. The dedication program for Ingels School said, "His untimely death took from this district a true professional whose organizational ability and exemplary leadership commanded the respect of his staff, his pupils and the public."

Built in 1968 at 8925 Longview Road, Smith-Hale became the third and last junior high school in the district. The school was named for two former Ruskin High School teachers: Mrs. Mabel Smith, who taught from 1945 to 1962 and Miss Mabel Hale, who taught from 1948 to 1964.

Santa Fe Accelerated Elementary School, at 8908 Old Santa Fe Road, is located on a former campsite of the Santa Fe Trail.

Moving to a new school involved a massive amount of planning. Occupancy of Santa Fe School was delayed due to a strike at the factory where the air conditioners were being made. Consequently, the move to the new school took place over the winter holidays, December 1970.

The process began on the 28th, with teachers and their classroom equipment and supplies coming in a prearranged schedule, beginning with Union Point, then Dobbs, Holmes Park, Johnson, Truman, Ingels, Longview Methodist Church, which also housed district students.

The Staff Bulletin #7, compiled to facilitate the move, provided precise plans: "Each child in your room will be furnished two shopping bags. Have them put all of their personal belongings and text books, EXCEPT READING, PHONICS, and WORKBOOKS, in these bags. Mark each child's bag with his name and new room number in large letters with magic marker.

"Third, fourth, fifth, sixth, Special Education V and VI will take these bags home with them on Tuesday and Wednesday evening and bring them back to Santa Fe on Jan. 4.

"Grades 1, 2, Sp. Ed. I, II, III, and IV will line them along the wall so the movers can move them. Special Education III and IV will take yours to the Ingels stage on Wednesday afternoon, December 23.

"Pack ALL workbooks and reading books in boxes marked with your name and new room number on the end of the box.

"You will be provided with masking tape, a magic marker, 10 cardboard boxes and shopping bags. If you find you need more boxes, use only boxes with lids so they can be stacked in the truck.

"All desks, students and teachers, and cabinets must be empty with the drawers taped shut. If you have keys for any of these things, tape them inside. DO NOT pack things inside your cabinets, files or bookshelves. (Exception – put your pencil sharpeners in your top file drawer.)

"ALL articles of furniture must be marked with a strip of masking tape and magic marker: mark student desks on the top; mark student chairs on the top of seat; mark teachers desks on top; mark teacher chair on top of seat; mark file cabinets on top drawer; mark metal cabinets on door; mark wooden book cases on top; mark maps on metal frame; mark globes on base (if you don't have a box for it).

"Any items not marked will not be moved."

Work on the unfinished building continued after classes began. Additions were made to the school during the next two years, and the dedication of the building was in 1972.

A Second High School

Election after election during the late 1960s, voters failed to pass bond issues requested by the school board. Finally, in 1971, due to an inadequate operating levy, Hickman Mills C-1 School District did not open until September 21. The previous spring district teachers had gone on strike to show their concern over the planned school-opening delay and to compel district leaders and voters to grant a pay increase. Until a court order forced them back to work, striking teachers picketed the district's administration building.

This was a time of general uncertainty.

In precincts throughout the country, Americans balked at increasing taxes. Their reluctance was fueled by high inflation, which persistently hovered at 10 percent or more annually during the 1970s. The economic forecast particularly threatened middle class Americans, such as those living in Hickman Mills.

In the face of difficult times, the school board of Hickman Mills C-1 School District continued to seek tax support from voters. The 13 schools – one high school and 12 elementary schools – were not enough to handle the enormous influx of new students arriving every year. Ruskin High School had almost 900 seniors – more than the entire school's enrollment when Ruskin was built a little more than 12 years earlier. The district needed additional school buildings, especially a new high school.

The election that finally succeeded in passing the levy required to build a second high school was unusual. It was the first one in the history of the school district in which 18 year olds had the opportunity to cast their votes in school district balloting.

According to a press release issued by Hickman Mills C-1 School District in 1972, "When Hickman Mills High School [at 9010 Old Santa Fe Road] opens for sophomores and juniors, it will contain 44 classrooms, a cafeteria with kitchen, a library, an auditorium type classroom for the use of debating and other speech and forensic activities, two gymnastic areas and one gymnasium…

"This school site…is located on the 'high prairie,' a campsite of the Santa Fe Trail. Using the westward movement as a general theme, the present sophomore class has selected the cougar as its mascot for the future school, and its school colors of white and burnt orange.

"Occupancy of Hickman Mills High School will end split sessions at Ruskin that were held last year and are being held the current school year."

In Fall, 1997, Hickman Mills C-1 School District became an A+ School. The high school also adopted a class period modification called "block scheduling," which designated the eighth period for a seminar period. Ruskin High School went to block scheduling the following year. In 1999, the district's middle schools (formerly called junior high schools) adopted the block schedule.

The crisis continued the next fall – even with the addition in 1972 of a 13th new grade school, Santa Fe Elementary School (now called Santa Fe Accelerated Elementary School). Increased overcrowding and lack of building funds forced the district to establish a split-shift schedule for Ruskin High School. The first shift started at 6 a.m., and the second ended at 7p.m.

Finally, after 14 levy elections, voters approved taxes for the school board's proposed building projects. On August 27, 1973, an unfinished Hickman Mills High School was opened. The multi-million dollar project represented two years of planning and another two years of construction. That year, Ruskin graduated 418 seniors. Down the road, at the largest school ever built by the district, 477 graduating seniors became the first to don the orange tassels of Hickman Mills High School.

According to a 1972 school district press release, "(T)he board conducted a contest in the school district asking patrons and pupils to submit suggested names for the new high school. After considering more than 50 names that were submitted, the board selected the name Hickman Mills High School submitted by Miss Pamela Jones [shown here], daughter of Mr. and Mrs. Joseph M. Jones...At that time she had just completed the sixth grade at Johnson Elementary School. She is currently a member of the junior class at Ruskin High School."

On her handwritten entry to the contest, Pamela explained her reason for picking the name, "We need to maintain our idenity [sic] as Hickman Mills."

Some of the other suggested names that did not win the contest included Mrs. Alta Guyll (the school nurse who died in the 1957 tornado); Ruskin North; Loma Vista; M.E. Langford; Blaine E. Steck; Lois Moore; Dred Scott; Mark Twain; Thomas Hart Benton; Francois Chouteau; William Becknell; John F. Kennedy; and Margaret E. Powell.

CHAPTER 8: THE JOURNEY INTO THE 21ST CENTURY

Dr. Marjorie Williams, current C-1 superintendent, and children from each of the district's elementary schools joined the groundbreaking ceremonies on April 20, 2001, for the new Triangle, the intersection of major interstate highways in southeast Kansas City. Students in the photograph are Tanyaneeka Bresette, Anthony Caldwell, Samer Ghani, Brian Harness, Jana LaMaster, Jerri McCoy, Justin Myrick and Briana Simmons. In 2000, Dr. Williams became the first African-American to serve as the district's superintendent.

Photograph by Terry Murphy-Latta

A Changing Curricula

By 1977, when Hickman Mills C-1 School District was 75 years old, the district had 1,500 high school students and offered more than 170 upper level courses.

In the early years of the district, high school courses primarily prepared students for college – as opposed to life. Life skills – for women: sewing, cooking, homemaking and for men: plowing and harvesting, farm management – were learned at home. Agricultural classes were aimed at university-bound students, not students seeking practical knowledge. When C-1 opened in 1902, public schools did not provide vocational training.

By the time the district celebrated its 75th anniversary, all that had changed.

The basics continued. English, history, math and science remained staples. But in the third quarter of the century, half-unit electives were an important part of the course menu. Courses with names such as Modern Novels, Language of the Film, and The Presidents replaced the old survey classes. In 1978, during a period of intense interest in environmental issues, the district received a grant for developing a new high school course called "Energy – Its Application and Conservation," which would be used as a model for other school districts. Four years earlier, Truman Elementary School's PTA helped create an Outdoor Educational Lab on the campus.

Until the 1957 tornado, the Administration Center, which included the Superintendent's office, was located at Burke Elementary School, prior to being at Ruskin High School. Following the storm, the office was moved to the cement-block building at the northwest corner of the Ruskin campus. That building was constructed almost entirely of the debris from the tornado. In the mid 1970s, as the district's administrative services expanded and the Ruskin campus building became crowded, additional space was rented from the Department of Instruction at 5735 Red Bridge Road.

In 1980, a new administration building was constructed, using an earth-covered design. The design maximized energy conservation and minimized vandalism. Located at 9000 Santa Fe Trail Road, the Administration Center occupies the same large acreage as Hickman Mills High School and Santa Fe Elementary School.

Rockford School was closed and sold to the Army Corps of Engineers in 1975. The land the school occupied was part of the site slated for the man-made, 4,830-acre Longview Lake. Four years later Holmes Park School also closed, after being used by the district's Department of Buildings & Grounds for a few years. It was then sold to Marion Laboratory on April 21, 1997. The two schools were later demolished.

The last two original grade schools, Union Point and Hickman School, closed in 1980. Today, in 2002, the two buildings are owned and operated by church communities.

A dramatic decline in enrollment was the key factor in closing the four century-old schools. But another reason, perhaps equally important, was the changes required in operating a viable school in the late 20th century. When the four brick buildings were built in 1916, electricity was not commonplace. In fact, Rockford was not wired for electricity until the 1935/36 school year. Even then its power line was merely spliced into the line of a neighboring farm (records refer to it as the "Hornbuckle place"). By the time the four schools closed, the electronic age had begun.

Hickman Mills C-1 School District was one of the first in the metropolitan area to recognize the enormous impact that electronic technology would have in the workplace, as well as at home, during the next century. In 1983, to increase computer knowledge and accessibility in the schools, the district launched a long-range plan to purchase computer equipment and software and to offer teacher-training workshops. Four years later, the district had 226 microcomputers dedicated to instruction and 16 additional computers ordered. At that time many of the schools had computer labs. As the long-range plan indicated, "The use of computers in the classrooms is infinite."

Through the years, new curricula departments were added: music, industrial arts, home economics, business and vocation education. As early as the 1930s students could take bookkeeping, shorthand and typing. Among the items purchased during the 1933/34 school year were four new typewriters, each costing $70. As office equipment became more and more complex, additional classes were added during the 1940s. With the Vocational Educational Act of 1963 students found an array of new courses from which to choose. State and federal funds allowed the schools to purchase entire classrooms of electric typewriters, calculators and transcribing equipment.

Education also moved beyond the classroom. By the mid-1950s Distributive Education, and later Trades and Industries, had joined the list of academic departments, featuring on-the-job training outside of the school. In 1972, another beyond-the-school-walls program called Office Occupations was added. Hundreds of students from the district signed on for the New Vocational-Technical School in Raytown. Many of the district's students attended the Joe Herndon Area Vocational Technical School.

When Ruskin High School, built after the 1957 tornado, opened for the school year 1958/59, these new courses were offered:

Communications	*Business Law*
Careers	*Drafting III*
Latin II	*Sheet Metal Working*
Crafts	*Related Arts*
Music Appreciation	*Physiology*
Sociology	*English IV*
Family Living	*Art III*

These former courses continued to be offered:

English I, II, III	*Algebra I, II*	*Bookkeeping*
Literature	*Plane Geometry*	*Shorthand*
Journalism	*Trigonometry*	*General Shop*
Citizenship	*Solid Geometry*	*Woodworking*
World History	*General Science*	*Drafting I, II*
American History	*Biology*	*Metalworking*
American Problems	*Chemistry*	*Art I, II*
American Government	*Physics*	*Home Economics I, II*
Missouri History	*Typing*	*Speech I, II*
Geography	*General Business*	*Dramatics*
Psychology	*Office Practice*	*Band*
General Math	*Secretarial Practice*	*Chorus*
Glee Club	*Physical Education*	

"The first duty of government is to see that people have food, fuel, and clothes. The second, that they have means of moral and intellectual education."

John Ruskin,
Fors Clavigera (1876), letter 67.

Crittenton Center is located at 10918 Elm.

What began as a single course in mechanical drawing in 1950 expanded into a multi-room complex, with room-sized power equipment for metal and wood-working students.

Performing arts – music and theater – played important roles in student activities. In the early 1940s, Ruskin had an orchestra, and students performed musicals and operettas. Gilbert and Sullivan's *Pinafore* and *Mikado* were perennial favorites. During the 1940s, Ruskin repeatedly won state championships in drama and debate competitions.The orchestra was eventually dropped, returning in the 1960s, but the band remained an important addition to both student performers and audiences.

Foreign language in 1902 meant Latin. Gradually that ancient language faded from the curricula until its reappearance in the fall of 1957. It remained a staple for 14 years when a scarcity of Latin teachers caused it to disappear again. Spanish was offered in the early 1950s and until 1957 was the only foreign language taught at Ruskin. At that time French was added, with German following at the end of the 1960s.

In 1975, Rockford Elementary School closed. As one of the original four schools to consolidate in 1902, the closing, and ultimately the razing of the building, was a solemn event, not unlike the passing of an old friend. The school was more than a landmark. For the generations of adults who attended the old school, it had been the silent but constant witness to their childhoods – to more than a century of childhoods.

Rockford closed because enrollment was dropping. In the early 1970s, student enrollment held at about 15,000. By 1979, more than 10,000 high school students had graduated from the district during the last 25 years. And yet in that same year, total enrollment numbers dropped to 10,410.

The Hickman Mills C-1 School District was not unusual. The decline reflected a nation-wide trend. Population experts offered many reasons...baby-boomer years were over...the population was aging...people were waiting longer to start their families...couples were having fewer children than previous generations.

Spofford Center, shown here, moved to its current location, at 9700 Grandview Road, in 1978.

In addition to these factors, the Hickman Mills community experienced a precipitous population reduction in 1977 when Richards-Gebaur Air Force Base shifted most of its work force to an air base in Illinois. Many parents in the district lost jobs. Some residents were forced to move in order to follow the job market.

In the years after the base closing, the district's enrollment declined steadily and more schools closed. Holmes Park School shut its doors in 1979, and the last two original grade schools from the 1902 consolidation, Union Point and Hickman Schools, closed the following year.

In the fall of 1980, with space now available in the less crowded school buildings, the district's kindergartens moved into the elementary schools. Through the years, due to overcrowding, the youngest students had met in various locations around the district, including several churches: Broadview (9100 Blue Ridge); Besonia (9906 East Bannister Road); Ruskin Way (111th Terr. and Ruskin Way); Longview (7201 Longview Rd.); Red Bridge (4901 Red Bridge Road); and Terrace Lake (4500 Red Bridge Rd.).

School closings continued. The next school year (1981/82), in a final report to the Executive Board at Westridge Elementary School, the board's historian, Judy Shute, wrote, "In March of this year the School Board and Administration decided to close two elementary schools and one junior high school in order to save money, and because of low enrollment. Those schools named were Johnson Elementary, Westridge Elementary and Baptiste Junior High. All three schools gave presentations on why their schools should not be closed. The decision was made anyway and Westridge students will go to Warford and Santa Fe Elementary Schools next year...

"It would be impossible to tell you all the grand things that have happened at Westridge since it opened, just as it would be to acknowledge all the wonderful teachers and PTA people who have made it all possible.

"We put up a good fight this year to keep our school open. We failed, but they cannot close our hearts – or take away our memories of Westridge."

Emotions ran high. It was easy to celebrate the opening of a new building, but quite difficult to watch an old one close.

A student in Management II School is shown here. The program uses community involvement and innovative curricula in an effort to provide mutual respect, opportunities for success, and to foster a sense of self-worth and dignity.

The students of Baptiste Day School are beneficiaries of a series of state and national laws that expanded access to educational opportunities.

In the Rehabilitation Act of 1973, the government linked compliance with funding. It barred discrimination against the disabled in any federally funded program, specifically requiring appropriate educational services for disabled children.

In 1974, Missouri's Law for Education of the Handicapped provided additional guidelines for the state's schools.

In 1975, Congress passed the Education for All Handicapped Children Act, prompting states to experiment with mainstreaming disabled students. The law, which guaranteed a "free, appropriate public education" for all disabled students, is now known as the Individuals with Disabilities Education Act. The law has been amended several times, most recently in 1997. The Americans With Disabilities Act, passed in 1990, bars all forms of discrimination against the disabled.

Despite the school closings, these years continued to be years of expansion. For the Hickman Mills C-1 School District, expansion in the last quarter of the 20th century meant expanding opportunities and educational equality. That equality meant extending education to include previously disenfranchised groups – minority groups, disabled, learning impaired. The goal was to ensure that all children have a chance at a full educational experience – a chance, in short, at a full life.

Equality of numbers – and equality of content. It was not enough to achieve balance and inclusion. What went on in the classroom had to continue to be relevant. And even more challenging, in a rapidly changing world, curricula needed to anticipate the needs of tomorrow's society and to prepare students to meet those needs. No less.

In the 1960s, Hickman Mills incorporated a wide range of services for children with special needs. During this time, the district's annual reviews pointed out, "Within our school population are those students whose education needs differ greatly from the majority of students. Their educational needs arise from their individuality – distinctively human – and cannot be met through school programs designed for the average students.

"They are the exception – the handicapped. Consequently they are often referred to as exceptional or handicapped children.

"By definition, handicapped or exceptional children are those who differ from the average to such a degree in physical, mental or psychological characteristics that the general school program does not afford them the opportunity for adequate achievement or acceptable adjustment. These children need either specialized instruction or supportive services or both, to achieve at a level commensurate with their respective abilities.

"For this reason, CSD-1 considers these children to be SPECIAL. They have special needs. Therefore, specialized instruction or supportive services were established to provide the exceptional or handicapped child with an equal opportunity to learn."

The U.S. Congress passed the Elementary and Secondary Education Act in 1965. Perhaps the most far-reaching education law of the 20th century, ESEA helped to propel a movement to improve schools and to spur a national dialogue on education standards. ESEA was the first federal funding program for local school districts, public and private. Some studies revealed that as districts began to comply with the law, federal spending on K-12 tripled between 1964 and 1966.

ESEA provided funding to advance the education of all disadvantaged children, including the disabled. Because the Civil Rights Act of 1964 barred racial discrimination in all federally funded programs, the law suddenly offered a powerful inducement for complying with Brown v. Board of Education. ESEA, in effect, took Brown and gave it muscle.

ESEA also provided assistance to schools with high concentrations of poor children.

Later amendments broadened the definition of those included within the law's purview. Title IX, Educational Amendments of 1972, for example, included provisions against discrimination of students based on gender.

To qualify for ESEA's Title I money, school districts had to show results. The government created the Title I Evaluation and Reporting System – also called TIERS. It required schools to evaluate their federal programs by using norm-referenced tests – which compare students to a national sample – and it contributed to the "substantial expansion" in the use of them throughout the decade. The testing element of the 1965 law sparked a nationwide movement that linked a child's education success to test scores.

More than a quarter of a century later, the broad impact of the 1965 law continues to evolve and influence educational policy at the local level. ESEA's influence will probably grow during the 21st century because, according to U.S. Census predictions, in most states, including Missouri, 30 percent of the population between the ages of 18 and 24 will be non-Euro-ethnic by 2010.

Opened in 1985, the Early Childhood Center was renamed in 2000 the Freda Markley Early Childhood Center, after its director.

Class size in the Early Childhood programs is limited to 12 children, with one certified teacher and at least one para-professional. Children participate in various activities throughout the day, including circle time, center time and small group and outdoor times. Field trips are planned during the year. Monthly "Parent and Children Together" meetings offer chances for parents and their children to learn together. Weekly and monthly newsletters keep parents informed of activities and learning opportunities.

Multi-age classes are part of the district's Early Childhood Special Education Program. Classes meet four days a week for three hours, with additional home visits.

Programs included Alternative Education, Drug & Alcohol Abuse Education, Functional Education, Guidance & Counseling, Health Programs, Hearing Impaired, Home Instruction, Learning Disabilities, Physically Limited (Orthopedically Handicapped - O.H.), Preschool Screening, Special Adjustment, Speech & Language Development and Visually Impaired.

Meeting the needs of special-needs children continues into the district's second century. In 2000, Hickman Mills launched the Baptiste Day School. The educational and therapeutic school provides special education students, grades two through 12, with an intensive program. The program has individualized educational and behavioral components for children who are experiencing severe problems in their school, home and community. Included in the day school are several comprehensive elements: behavior management, small group instruction, individual and group counseling, family support and the services of a consulting psychiatrist. Day School's primary purpose is to prepare students for a successful return to the regular school environment as quickly as possible.

Beginning with the 1979/80 school year, Crittenton School, serving troubled youth, grades kindergarten through 12, became part of the Hickman Mills district. At that time, mostly long-term, residential students were part of the program. Later, day students were also enrolled from Hickman Mills, as well as surrounding districts. Beginning in 1999/2000, Crittenton again served only long-term, residential students, with the day students attending Baptiste Day School and the short-term students being served by their home schools.

Spofford School joined the district's community of education equality programs during the same year that Crittenton joined. Founded as an orphanage in 1916, Spofford's role in helping children has changed through the years. Today its mission is to treat the entire family.

In 1998, the district opened its Management II School. The school's basic assumption is that behavior is a set of skills that can be taught and learned. Believing that early detection is the key for acquiring these skills, Management II teaches children social, behavioral and education skills necessary for successful integration into a regular classroom setting, as well as for graduation and employment. Management II offers a safe, supportive and nurturing educational/social environment for at-risk students who have not succeeded in traditional classroom settings.

In April 1983, the U.S. Department of Education's National Commission on Excellence in Education issued a report that reviewed the country's educational systems. Called *A Nation At Risk*, the influential and controversial report concluded, "The educational foundations of our society are presently being eroded by a rising tide of mediocrity that threatens our very future as a nation and a people. We have, in effect, been committing an act of unthinking, unilateral educational disarmament."

The report reflected a widespread concern about the health of the country's public schools. Many large districts, mostly in the nation's cities, faced a multitude of challenges caused by rapid changes in enrollment and curriculum standards, which were being mandated at both the state and national levels. Although an urban district, Hickman Mills C-1 School District was a small educational system, allowing the district to quickly identify and readily implement programs to meet the needs of all of its children.

Two years prior to the DOE Commission's report, the school board wrote in its 1981 Annual Review & Budget Information: "Self-evaluation and precise long-range planning – key factors and commitments by the district in an effort to maintain a quality educational program – are no longer just desirable, they are now imperative.

"The acceleration of change in demographics, financing, and technology is staggering. Inter-governmental relationships, legal interpretations, regulations and compliance requirements create a constantly changing maze which must be conquered day after day in order to apply what strength remains to education issues."

Of course, meeting the needs of all children means creating a stimulating classroom environment for high-ability children. To that end, the district launched intensive enrichment programs in 1981. The three programs were directed toward the gifted and talented students. Center Of Differentiated Education (CODE) focuses on grades four through 12, while Primary Enrichment Program (PEP) works with younger students, kindergarten through third grades. Artistic and Creative Exploration (ACE) meets the needs of children, grades one through six, who demonstrate exceptional ability in one or more artistic areas.

Children in the district's three gifted education programs, Center Of Differentiated Education (CODE) [shown here], Primary Enrichment Program (PEP), and Artistic and Creative Exploration (ACE) spend the entire day, one day a week, at the Baptiste Educational Center. All three programs are designed to address specific standards outlined by the Missouri Department of Elementary and Secondary Education. In September each year, the selection process for enrollment in the programs begins. The process starts by formulating a pool of potentially qualified students who will then proceed through a step-by-step admissions procedure.

Students who have classes at Baptiste Educational Center are transported from their home schools to the center.

In 1985, the district initiated the Parents As Teachers program. PAT is designed to help parents sharpen their parenting skills and to assist youngsters in growing physically, mentally and socially through their critical years of child development. This early childhood program provides parent education for parents with young children from birth to five years of age. Home visits and group meetings offer opportunities for both the parent and child. Besides assisting parents with child development issues, the program provides screening services throughout the year, which help detect potential health problems, disabilities, or delays that could interfere with a child's learning and development.

Studies have shown that children whose parents participate in the PAT program score higher on tests of intelligence, achievement, language ability and positive social development than do comparison groups.

In 1991, the district offered an additional component to its early childhood program. Ages three through five were served four days a week and three hours a day in the district's Early Childhood Special Education program. Home visits with parents and children was also part of the program.

The following year, the early childhood program expanded to include Title I Preschool. It serves children with identified educational needs one and two years before they begin kindergarten.

The need for these programs was so great that there was soon a waiting list for enrollment. Consequently in 1997, Friday School was added to the Early Childhood program. This class serves children who are one year away from kindergarten and on the waiting list for the Title 1 preschool.

During the last year of the 20th century, a new program was added. Called the Missouri Preschool Project Grant, it meets the needs of children one and two years away from kindergarten with identified educational needs. Children in the program receive preschool experience through a partnership with two community day programs. The grant covers the cost of the three-day, four-hour-per-day program.

Warford Elementary School was one of 17 area schools chosen to participate in the CowParade Kansas City 2001. More than 200 painted cows, including Warford's Westward Ho! [shown here], were on exhibit on the streets of greater Kansas City during the spring and summer of 2001. Warford's colorful, life-sized fiberglass cow was on display at Union Station, with several other entries in the citywide art event.

Westward Ho! now lives in a small community in eastern Missouri, which purchased the cow in an auction held on the internet during the fall of 2001. Sales of the 200+ painted cows benefited the educational programs at three area non-profit organizations: American Royal Association, Kansas City Zoological Park and Kemper Museum of Contemporary Art.

The entire enrollment of Hickman Mills C-1 School District, which had continued to drop during the 1980s, began to stabilize in the early 1990s. Consequently, programs such as Baptiste Day School, PEP/CODE/ACE, Crittenton, Spofford, Freda Markley Early Childhood Center and Management II School seemed certain to grow during the next century.

In 1995, there were 7,093 students enrolled in the district, which included eight grade schools, two middle schools, two high schools and more than a dozen special programs. Each year thereafter, the enrollment numbers increased. In 1990, Johnson Elementary School, which had been leased to the Marion Laboratory Company after its closing in 1982, was used as the Johnson Educational Center. Nine years later, due to the district's growing number of students, it was gutted and rebuilt from the inside out and reopened again as an elementary school.

Since the years following the 1930s Depression, when a shortfall of funds prompted previously self-sufficient local districts to seek financial help on the state level, the role of setting education policy began shifting more and more to state officials. After the 1960s, that role continued up the governmental ladder to Washington, D.C. Through the 1960s and 1970s, legislative action on the state and national levels had an enormous impact on education policy. Affirmative action laws provided guidelines for enrollment goals. Assessment standards influenced curriculum decisions. Bit by bit, the once autonomous local school districts yielded their decision-making powers – whether on matters of finances, building construction, curricula or testing – to a centralized education policy maker.

Prior to A Nation At Risk, state governments played minor roles in curricula matters. After 1983, state officials not only began reviewing classroom content, but defining it as well. Today, except for Idaho and Iowa, every state has established statewide curriculum standards in at least one subject. In addition, many states, Missouri included, have created assessment and comprehensive accountability programs designed to ensure that those standards are met.

Missouri's Excellence in Education Act of 1985 provided the framework in which all Missouri schools were mandated to use a criterion-referenced test to measure directly student mastery of key skills. Those skills were identified by Missouri educators, and the tests were developed within Missouri. The test, Missouri Mastery and Achievement Tests, focused on four broad skill areas: Language Arts/Reading/English; Mathematics; Science; and Social Studies/Civics.

In 1993, the Missouri legislature passed the Outstanding Schools Act, which led to the creation of the Missouri Assessment Program (MAP). All public schools in the state are required to implement the performance-based assessment system, which is designed to assess student progress toward meeting the Show-Me Standards. Those standards consist of 73 rigorous content and performance standards adopted by the State Board of Education in January 1996.

Students are required to have strong knowledge and skills in basic subject areas. The six areas are Mathematics, Communication Arts, Science, Social Studies, Health/Physical Education and Fine Arts. MAP measures what a student knows as well as what he or she can do. Achievement levels on the MAP are identified using four categories: Progressing, Near Proficient, Proficient and Advanced.

Hickman Mills C-1 School District started using MAP, beginning with the math assessment, in the spring of 1997. Each year thereafter a new area was added.

With one eye on the mandates of government and the other on the needs of the local community – a community that covers 32 square miles with a population of approximately 52,300 people – the Hickman Mills C-1 School District, its board, administrators, educators and parents steer their way through a multitude of challenges. In many ways, the path is made easier by experience – one hundred years of experience. A long history with many lessons.

And what is history but the yardstick by which we measure our progress? It is the way we take stock of what we have done, how well we have done it and how we might fashion our future in order to do better. Within any one-hundred-year period, events of great triumph are certain to occur. Events of great trial, too.

A century yardstick is, therefore, a measurement in and of itself. It says, "We've stood the test of time – a long, long time." A century of history is also a hard taskmaster. It demands that we succeed, that we carry on, that we not lose faith with those who came before us. It challenges us to keep the torch burning for the ones to come.

And for all those, past, present and future, we are bound together by the forces of history.

Our history. The journey we follow to a promising future.

Acknowledgments

Special thanks to:

Ben Ervin for sharing his extensive knowledge of the district's early years, for providing enlightening tours and for his unfailing enthusiasm and humor.

J.B. Brown for offering his encouragement and collection of historic photographs and documents related to the Hickman Mills community.

Marge Langford for sharing her memories of living and working in the Hickman Mills C-1 School District.

Roy Becklean and Blaine Steck for their insight into the school district's mid-century years.

Roscoe Bernard for sharing his memories about Baptiste Junior High School and his work with the Harmon Bus Company.

Harold Lorimer for providing invaluable information related to Woodman Hall and the early years of the district's history.

Nancy Terwilliger for generously contributing the Slaughter family's collection of historic photographs and documents.

Robert and Gay-linn Gatewood for sharing their family's history.

Terry Murphy-Latta for her generous help and for sharing her contemporary photographs related to the district's history.

Dr. Sharon Slusher for her cheerful guidance.

Mildred Harness and Jean Freeman for their research contributions.

Sandy Diehl and Linda Wilson for writing the history of Truman Elementary School.

Ralph Smith for offering materials related to the Hickman Mills Community Christian Church and the Jacob Palmer family.

Wayne Flaherty for providing information related to the historic trails that pass through the school district.

Jim Parkison for his help with research related to post-World War II housing developments.

The Hickman Mills C-1 School District Public Information Office staff Curt Heeney, Kelly Kalinka, Dana Terry and Jan Perry, for their on-going support and help.

The members of the History Committee for the Centennial Celebration: Dr. Sharon Slusher, Teresa Edens, David Odneal, Lee Nelson, Scott Jennings, Roger Williams, Jan Perry and Terry Murphy-Latta, for their dedication to preserving the history of Hickman Mills C-1 School District.

The district wishes to thank Ms. Jami Parkison, author of this documentary of our history. Ms. Parkison has provided us with an appreciation of our past through both her professional and personal commitment to this project. We appreciate how she has touched our lives and has supported us throughout this most important year in our journey.

Book production by
Acorn Books, Kansas City, Missouri.

Book layout and design by
Stonehouse Studio, Shirley Marriott Harryman
(1974 Ruskin High School graduate)
Kansas City, Missouri.

Contributors to the Production of
The Journey To Our Future

Trailblazer ($1,000 and above)
Aventis Pharmaceuticals
485 Properties, LLC (Bannister Mall)

Wagonmaster ($500 and above)
Buffet Garden
Big T's Bar B-Q

Homesteader ($250 and above)
Hickman Mills C-1 School District Board of Education 2001-2002
Dr. Marjorie Williams
Dr. Sharon Retschlag-Slusher
Ruskin Heights Homes Association, Inc.

Pioneer ($100 or above)
Betty Akers
Fred Albright /Albright Chevrolet
Dobbs Elementary School PTA 2001-2002
Dobbs Elementary School Staff 2001-2002
Jim and Teresa Edens
Ben Ervin
Dr. Harold Frye
Hickman Mills High School Staff 2001-2002
Hickman Mills NEA
Barbara Hulett
Humana, Inc.
Johnson Elementary School PTA 2001-2002
Johnson Elementary School Staff 2001-2001
George and Betty Kolb
Terry Murphy-Latta and John Latta
Liston Insurance
Jenee Lowe
Debra Nelson
Virginia Ervin Parker
John and Jami Parkison
Jan Perry
Bob Rethemeyer
St. Luke's United Methodist Church
St. Matthew Apostle Church
Santa Fe Accelerated Elementary School Staff 2001-2001
Topper Schumacher Family
Smith-Hale Middle School Staff and PTSA 2001-2002
Blaine and Audrey Steck
Charlotte Slaughter Terwilliger
Roger C. Williams Jr.
Southern Communities Coalition

BIBLIOGRAPHY

An Illustrated Historical Atlas Map of Jackson County, Mo. Brink, McDonough & Co., Philadelphia, 1877.

Brewer, Carolyn Glenn. **Caught in the Path. A Tornado's Fury, a Community's Rebirth. The Ruskin Heights Tornado, May 20, 1957.** Prairie Fugue Books, Kansas City, Missouri, 1997.

Castel, Albert. **William Clarke Quantrill: His Life and Times.** The General's Books, Columbus, Ohio, 1992.

Connelley, William Elsey. **The Life of Preston B. Plumb, 1837-1891.** Browne & Howell Company, Chicago, Illinois, 1913.

County and City Data Book, 1972. U.S. Department of Commerce. Bureau of Census, 1972.

Diehl, Sandra and Linda Wilson. **Harry S Truman Elementary School, 1956-1996, Celebrating 40 Years of Progress.** Privately published, 1996. [56-page booklet]

Dorsett, Lyle Wesley. **"Slaveholding in Jackson County, Missouri."** March 1962.[Native Sons of Kansas City Prize in Local History, established by Carl Lowenstein in 1960.]

Eakin, Joanne C. and Donald R. Hale. **Branded As Rebels.** Wee Print, Independence, Missouri, 1993.

Ervin, Ben. **"Comments Concerning the History of Hickman Mills Community Christian Church."** Printed in Celebration of the Congregation's 156th Birthday. May 20, 2001. [11 page paper.]

Goff, William A. **"The First Battle of Westport, June 17, 1863."** *Westport Historical Quarterly*. March 1970.

Greene, Lorenzo J., Gary R. Kremer and Antonio F. Holland. **Missouri's Black Heritage.** Revised and updated by Gary R. Kremer and Antonio F. Holland. University of Missouri Press, 1993.

Hickman, W.Z. **History of Jackson County, Missouri.** Historical Publishing Company, 1902. New material added, published by Southern Historical Press, Inc., 1990.

Hicks, John Edward. **"Civil War Ordeal for Hickman Mills."** *Kansas City Times*. August 25, 1969.

Jefferys, Charles P. B. **"The Jefferys Family at Blithedale."** A speech given before the Old Settlers Club, Hickman Mills, Kansas City, Missouri, September 26th, 1969. [Nine page paper.]

Kemper, Harvey H. **"History of Hickman Mills."** 1983. [16 page paper]

Palmer, Jacob Teaford. **"A Jackson County Citizen Writes of the Time of Quantrell's [sic] and the Jayhawkers."** *Belton Herald*, Local History section, 1911.

Ragan, Mrs.Greenberry. **"A Panoramic of the Lost Townships."** Jackson County Historical Society, December 1965.

Schirmer, Sherry Lamb and Richard D. McKinzie. **At the River's Bend: An Illustrated History of Kansas City.** Windsor Publications, Inc., Woodland Hills, California, 1982. Produced in association with the Jackson County Historical Society.

Scott Sr., Mrs. Harry, Mrs. J. M. Slaughter and Miss Mae Pennington. **History of the Hickman Mills Community Christian Church, 1845-1945.** Printed by Rhoadschnellpresse [sic], Inc. First edition, 1965.

Slaughter, Stephen S. **"The Early Years of the Hickman Mills Community Christian Church."** February 1986. [41 page paper]

Slaughter, Stephen S. **History of a Missouri Farm Family. The O.V. Slaughters, 1700-1944.** Harbor Hills Books, Harrison, New York, 1978.

"Twilight Twister" The Dramatic Picture Story of South Jackson County's Darkest Hours. *Jackson County Advocate*, Grandview, Missouri, 1977.